PRAISE FOR JEFF COEN'S

Family Secrets: The Case That Crippled the Chicago Mob

"Revealing, shocking. . . . Superbly crafted, this is a tragic, clear-sighted account of how Chicago's mighty mob was brought to heel."

—*Publishers Weekly*

"[An] authoritative account of one of the most amazing Chicago Outfit cases in history . . . indispensable."

—John Kass, columnist, *Chicago Tribune*

"A telling look inside the twisted world of organized crime."

—*Kirkus Reviews*

"Moves with the urgency of a can't-put-it-down novel."

—Rick Kogan, author, journalist, and radio host

"A stellar recounting of the . . . systematic dismantling of the Chicago Outfit."

—*Men's Book*

"Reads like a fast-paced crime thriller . . . fascinating reading."

—*Times* (Northwest Indiana)

"Like a true-life *Sopranos*, complete with life-and-death drama, *Family Secrets* is a story of crime, corruption and the subterranean streams of money that built fortunes and sucked life from entire sectors of society."

—*Shepherd Express* (Milwaukee)

PRAISE FOR JEFF COEN AND JOHN CHASE'S

Golden: How Rod Blagojevich Talked Himself Out of the Governor's Office and into Prison

"All those interested in the Blago drama or political intrigue in general can dive into this book with relish."

—*Publishers Weekly*, starred review

"Through indefatigable reporting and deft writing, [Coen and Chase] take us into a fascinating, Byzantine world of Chicago politics and power that largely goes unseen."

—David Mendell, author of *Obama: From Promise to Power*

"[Coen and Chase] offer a nuanced context of political corruption overlaid with Blagojevich's extraordinarily flamboyant personality, from the profanity to the hair obsession and outsized ego."

—*Booklist*

"*Golden* presents complicated political machinations in plain-facts terms, accessible to readers of all backgrounds. Highly recommended . . . to anyone interested in learning what really drove the Blagojevich scandal."

—*Midwest Book Review*

"The most ambitious book yet on the former governor's spectacular rise and fall."

—*Chicago Tribune*

MURDER
IN
CANARYVILLE

MURDER
IN
CANARYVILLE

THE TRUE STORY BEHIND A
COLD CASE AND A CHICAGO COVER-UP

JEFF COEN

CHICAGO
REVIEW
PRESS

Published by Chicago Review Press Incorporated
814 North Franklin Street
Chicago, Illinois 60610
ISBN 978-1-64160-281-5

Library of Congress Control Number: 2020946265

Interior design: Jonathan Hahn
Photo of John R. Hughes courtesy of the Hughes family

Printed in the United States of America
5 4 3 2 1

For Tracy and Sloane

And in memory of John R. Hughes

CONTENTS

Author's Note   *xiii*

Prologue. I

1 Boyce Field 6

2 The Friend 14

3 A Visit with the FBI 23

4 A Case to Look Into 34

5 The Gorman File 47

6 The Eyewitness 65

7 Digging In 78

8 Martha 97

9 The South Side Group 108

10 The Last Greylord Judge 127

11 A Green Chevrolet 138

12 A Sick Feeling 148

13 Haberkorn 157

14 The Cop 162

15 A Troubling Legacy 177

16 A Final Push 205

17 "I Really Want to Go Now" 216

Epilogue 229

Acknowledgments   *235*
Additional References   *237*

AUTHOR'S NOTE

Source material for this book comes primarily from interviews with the family and friends of John Hughes; interviews with retired police officers; police records and reports; author research and conversations with confidential sources; federal court records and transcripts; and materials written and gathered primarily by retired Chicago police detective Jim Sherlock, while he was working for the FBI.

Attempts have been made to stay as close to the official record as possible, though the official record is at times limited, and perhaps intentionally so.

Those limits are especially apparent in the official Chicago Police Department file, which was used by the author. Items that were gathered in a separate collection of material recovered by Sherlock, which became known as "the Gorman file," are noted as such; they include police records not found in the official file. That paperwork originally was gathered by James Gorman and attorney Brian Gilmartin. Eventually it was entered into the official CPD record by Sherlock, as described in the following pages.

Direct quotes from reference materials, including published news accounts and books, are noted in the text where they are made. Other reference items that were helpful to the project are listed later in the "Additional References" section at the end of the book.

Quotes from interviews and police reports are cited as such.

Quotes taken from police reports are also described according to which report is being used in the text and which file it was kept in. Those quotes are as close to the original material as possible. However, since such police reports are notorious for their misspellings, abbreviations, and accepted shorthand, some efforts have been made to smooth out those quotes for the reader without changing the original meaning of what was written. That is to say that obvious spelling errors have been corrected in the text without a "[*sic*]" note so as not to constantly distract from the narrative. Major changes for clarity include paraphrasing in a few instances, but again, not to a level that would change the meaning of the quotation.

Additionally, in two cases, names of individuals in this book have been fictionalized. Both fictional names are indicated by the use of SMALL CAPS on first mention. This decision was made in fairness to those people, as they found themselves under some scrutiny in a criminal investigation but have not been formally charged with any crimes. Any similarity between the fictionalized names and the names of other real people is strictly coincidental. In other instances, the proper names of some who were interviewed by investigators have simply been excluded or replaced with general descriptions. This was done for similar reasons, and in an effort not to unfairly lead to the identification of the two people whose names were fictionalized.

PROLOGUE

Jim Sherlock sat in a black Jeep Cherokee on a residential street in a town more than fifty miles from Chicago.

The SUV was unmarked, but he had made sure to use a vehicle that you could see had bars of emergency lights lined inside its windows, if you had a reason to look a little closer.

Months of peeling open aging records, jogging the memories of crusty old cops, and finding people who still remembered what happened, and here Sherlock was. There was little more to do than slip the Cherokee into park and watch. The house and the street were still. A typical street in a typical town just beyond the outer reaches of suburbia. The concrete had given way to subdivisions, which had given way to corn, which had given way to this.

He was a Chicago police detective. And yes, people always stopped on his name when he identified himself on the street or at the start of interviews. "Detective Sherlock?" they would say. "Right. You'll have to do better than that, pal. Where's Watson?"

He didn't blame them. He had made the jokes himself on occasion.

For years he had been on loan to the FBI, including a stint working cold cases, and for months he had been obsessed with this one. It would be his very last before retirement. It involved a murder four decades earlier, in a neighborhood that he knew well. It had ripped a teenager from his Irish American family and broken them. It was a family not unlike the one Sherlock himself had grown up in.

In many ways, Sherlock knew he was pulling on his final thread. He needed the man in the house to talk to him and tell him about a night more than forty years earlier. The car. The park. The gun. Sherlock believed the man held the key to the case that had proven to be among the most challenging and the most remarkable of his career. He believed dark forces at the intersection of Chicago government, police, and organized crime had worked to keep justice from being done, and he was out to change that.

But Sherlock's time with a badge was running out. He would need to work quickly to see this file stamped SOLVED before going on vacation, or moving on to the next stage of his life.

In any event, there was a very good chance the man in the house would already know what this was about and why an undercover police vehicle was sitting on his street. He had probably heard that the case that had dogged him for so many years had been reopened—again.

That was the way the neighborhoods worked.

Start asking questions, especially about a case like this one, and word traveled like an electric pulse across the grid of streets and alleys of Canaryville and Bridgeport. Through the family networks. Through the churches. Through the brick taverns and corner stores. Sherlock had been amazed how quickly he had gotten to the point at which he would call someone about the case and the person on the line would say someone already had told them Sherlock was poking around. Within days. Probably hours. So by now the information relay had almost certainly made it even here, to the town where the man Sherlock was watching now lived. This man had picked up and left Canaryville and Bridgeport for good long ago.

That was not the way the neighborhoods worked.

PROLOGUE

Clans there spread across generations, and roots ran deep. Irish, Italian, and Croatian families had ridden out good times and bad in Canaryville and Bridgeport and had stayed through the '60s and '70s, when African Americans began to move in great numbers into areas around them. The White youths had met that perceived threat with curses and rocks. It was a sad history that carried back to the city's 1919 race riots, which saw many hundreds of people killed in the area in clashes sparked by the drowning of a Black teen whose raft had drifted too close to a South Side beach claimed by Whites. To many, the neighborhoods were a fortress against a changing city, and they have long been key geography in Chicago's ongoing struggles with racism.

To most Chicagoans, Bridgeport was an ancestral stronghold of sorts, and a political enclave that was synonymous with the Daleys. But mention many other family surnames in these neighborhoods and their longtime residents could also tell you the street each of those families lived on, whom their kids hung out with in grade school, and probably which mass they attended. That was the real fabric. Politics, yes. But family first.

Even in the new century, these neighborhoods are old Chicago. That old city fades but never completely weathers away. It's there in the bricks peeking from a newly opened pothole. There in a painted sign for a long-closed business that slowly disappears on a building. And there in the phantom rail tracks that appear on a side street, forever headed to nowhere.

And of course it is there in the faces and voices of those who lived in Chicago long before meatpackers gave way to tech lofts, the world's largest Starbucks moved to Michigan Avenue, and international tourists appeared in droves to take selfies in front of a polished metal bean.

The Canaryville and Bridgeport of 1976 were not so glossy. They sat on the near Southwest Side, where Chicago's work got

3

done. Canaryville was believed to be so named for the swarms of small birds that once flocked to the old Union Stock Yards, where untold millions of hogs and cattle were gathered in a sea of pens and butchered for shipment across America. The neighborhood was home to tidy blocks of bungalows and two-flats owned by laborers, many of them Irish, and functioned more like its own town. Many residents knew as youngsters where they would go to church their whole lives and where they would be buried. The city's foundation grew here. They were proud of it.

Bridgeport, too, gave its sweat to the yards. Its history is filled with tales of Chicago laborers, many of them immigrants, who toughed out challenging conditions in their new city to make a path for their families. Some historians note that one of the area's first place names was telling enough: "Hardscrabble," which could have described Bridgeport for decades. It grew up along the Illinois and Michigan Canal before becoming a political seat of power for the Daleys.

Those, of course, are some of the better things that can be said about it. It was also insular to a fault. "It's a suspicious neighborhood," legendary Chicago columnist Mike Royko wrote of it in 1971 in his seminal book *Boss*: "a blend of Irish, Lithuanian, Italian, Polish, German, and all White. In the bars, heads turn when a stranger comes in. Blacks pass through in cars, but are unwise to travel by on foot."

Celebrations in 1976 marked the United States bicentennial. The Sears Tower already spiked above the Loop in the distance as a sign of things to come, but lifelong residents of Canaryville and Bridgeport who were senior citizens that year had lived as children in the Chicago of Al Capone.

No, the secrets would not come easily. Jim Sherlock knew it, and that was fine. Lost causes are the only ones worth fighting for, Clarence Darrow supposedly once said. Maybe that's what this was. Whatever truth was buried here, whatever the streets of Bridgeport and Canaryville would dish out, he would take. He was as Chicago as they were—in some ways the perfect person to take this up and not look back.

The town where Sherlock found himself that day in 2019 was called Sandwich, and the name was fitting. He wanted the man in the house across the street from where the undercover car was parked to feel like he was in one.

Sherlock had already spoken to the town's police chief to let him know what he would be doing there. He had told the chief the man was no real danger to anyone, and Sherlock needed no help or backup. The idea was to be seen and to shake up his target, make him think the investigation was much larger and more active than it was. The man inside the house might start to wonder why this unfamiliar SUV was sitting across from his home, and when the man took a moment to look more closely, he would realize it was a police vehicle.

In fact, this wasn't the only car Sherlock had used to sit in roughly this spot, hoping it would seem like multiple officers were on a rotating surveillance detail. It had been a silver Dodge on a prior visit. He was hopeful but not sure it was working, or if it would make any difference at all.

But cases like this one—the stubborn ones that lodge themselves in Chicago lore and stay there—those were the ones that were worth the work. Worth the months sifting through dusty files. Worth sitting in a car for hours and doing nothing.

Well, not always nothing. Sometimes Sherlock made it look like he was taking notes or jotting down something important, just in case his target was watching. He glanced out the Cherokee's window to check the house again.

Sherlock wanted the man inside to look.

The drapes moved.

I

BOYCE FIELD

Music spilled from the house party on Throop Street, common for a Friday night in the Bridgeport neighborhood. It was May, and Chicago high schools were wrapping up their academic years. Prom had been the prior weekend for many. It was still cool enough for jackets, but summer was starting to beckon.

Word had spread quickly that someone's parents were out of town and there was beer. Soon cars were pulling up filled with teens from the neighborhood and other blocks nearby. Their families were mostly Catholic, so they went to all-boys parochial schools with names like De La Salle and Leo, or to Maria, a nearby all-girls counterpart. De La Salle in particular reflected the political power of the area, as it eventually would be the alma mater of no less than five Chicago mayors, including both Mayor Daleys and Michael Bilandic.

A house party like the one that night would often mix teens from the neighborhoods, including some who were anything but friends. Groups of mostly Irish kids from Canaryville sometimes found themselves feuding with groups of mostly Italian kids from Bridgeport. It had been this way for most of their lives, though many of them did not know why. Had their parents or grandparents competed for the same blue-collar jobs as immigrants? Had the insular nature of their blocks naturally led to strife with other ethnic groups?

The foundations of the rift had long been buried by time, but it was real.

To those living with it that night in 1976, the division of the groups at times defied logic. Many of the teens went to school together and played together on the same sports teams. But out on the street, tensions were constant. Fistfights occurred regularly along Irish-Italian lines. Most teens from one side or the other had a story about the time their rivals had jumped them or their brother or friend. Many had tales of walking through neighborhood parks and narrowly escaping an ambush.

In fact, each side had a particular park that they held as a sort of home base. For the Italians, it was McGuane Park in Bridgeport, near Twenty-Ninth and Halsted. It was their hangout, and it was just a few blocks from the house party drawing kids together that night. For the Irish, it was Boyce Field, less than two miles to the south, in Canaryville. That park was just a couple of blocks from the longtime border between the two neighborhoods, Thirty-Ninth Street, or Pershing Road. It wasn't even a mile to the southwest of what was then called Comiskey Park, the home of the Chicago White Sox.

The reasons teens gathered at parties like this one were nothing new. The boys knew girls would be there and vice versa. There was laughter and the occasional sound of an empty beer bottle clattering above the blaring guitar chords of Led Zeppelin. The girls wore tight jeans and feathered their hair like Farrah Fawcett. Many of the boys grew their hair until it touched the oversized collars of the shirts under their leather jackets.

And it wasn't for a terribly new reason that tempers eventually would flare either: the wrong boy talking to the wrong girl. On this night it was apparently an Irish teen who spent a minute too long talking to one of the Italian girls, and her boyfriend didn't care for it. Pushing and shoving ensued inside the house at first, followed by shouting and more shoving in the front yard. Many teens at the party had seen this before and knew how it would go. Chest-puffing and alcohol would lead to punches being thrown and the cops getting called. Many of them decided they'd had enough before that started and began to make their way to their cars.

They knew the shoving and threats at the party meant they were probably in for a night of street fighting wherever the two groups found each other, and they were up for it. A group of six or seven Irish kids, including the teen who had talked to the girl, piled into one car and headed for Halsted.

Soon they circled up toward McGuane Park, intending to mess with whatever Italian kids they might find there. It was already 11:30 PM, but they were far from ready to pack it in for the night. When they reached the park, some of their longtime enemies had in fact made it there, and there was more shouting. The Irish kids pulled away.

They hadn't gone far before one of them glanced back out the rear window of their car. They were being followed. A larger group of Italian kids had jumped into two or three cars and were coming up fast. Clearly whatever offense had been taken at the party was not going to fade quickly, and they had made it worse by cruising near the park.

Might as well get it over with was the agreement among the Irish kids, who were more than willing to settle this with their knuckles. A few of the teens were especially skilled fighters and were not scared at the prospect of being outnumbered, which was what this skirmish was going to entail. They stopped their car on Halsted and quickly hopped out into the street.

The Italian kids did the same, and there were more than a dozen of them. Soon the two groups were punching each other and tearing at jackets. One of the Italians carried a small souvenir Go Go White Sox baseball bat, which was soon knocked from his

8

hands. Cars honked as the oblivious teenagers pounded each other in the street. One Irish youth was confronted by a group of four or five Italians when he was separated from his pack. He ran down a nearby alley and the Italians followed, evening the odds back on Halsted a bit.

In the chaos, one of the Italian kids was beaten over the head with the small White Sox bat. The groups only scattered and went back to their cars when someone caught sight of the police approaching.

The Irish kids had cuts and bruises, but they laughed as the Italians scrambled away. Things still weren't over, however. Someone being cracked over the head with what amounted to a club had only escalated things further, and both sides knew they were going to fight again. The Italians retreated to McGuane Park, while the Irish headed south, back toward Canaryville and Boyce Field.

On this night—as it was on most when the weather was good—Boyce was the center of the social system for the Irish kids of the neighborhood. The ending of the Throop Street house party and others in the area meant everyone was on their way there. On many nights, the boys might play pickup basketball while the girls watched. Many would sit on their cars with the doors open, listening to music from the stereo. There was certainly beer and couples sneaking off to hidden spots in the park.

The police would sometimes roll through but typically wouldn't roust the kids. They might take the beer from the underage teens, though. "Thanks, fellas. Captain's birthday tonight," they would laugh, putting a stray six-pack into their squad car.

The Irish boys from the fight on Halsted arrived to find the typical scene. Lines of cars were parked on the street beside the park, with friends sitting on their hoods and trunks. Some teens could be seen milling on the softball field nearby, drinking and laughing. But there was some tension. Word had spread about the fight and the fact that the Italians had been embarrassed. They had been turned back by the Irish teens despite outnumbering them, and one of their own had been hurt. They would surely be back with more people, maybe even raiding Boyce Field for a larger brawl. Irish kids there began to tell each other to make sure they knew how to get to their softball bats quickly, which many of them kept in their cars for weekend games. Some went ahead and got their bats out and sat them an arm's reach away.

There was a thought of taking the fight back to the Italians. Rumors of locations swirled in the park, places where some thought another fight might present itself.

Bands of friends talked about leaving and looking for the fight. If one broke out, they didn't want to leave the teens from their neighborhood out there without them. It was clear the Italians would only circle back with a much larger group. Some of the Irish kids got into one of their cars to head them off. But it wasn't to be. The teen whose car it was did not want to leave the park and go get in a fight, at least not on this night. He knew his car wouldn't turn over if it was in neutral, so as the friends talked of heading out, he slipped the gearshift down silently. The car didn't start, so the group decided to stick around.

For a time, it was quiet. Midnight had passed. Some in the park had started to grow more relaxed, joking around more than keeping watch. Maybe the Italians had thought better of making a trip into enemy territory.

"Car," someone said.

It wasn't clear who saw it first, but it was starting to attract attention. It was a light green Chevrolet sedan, maybe an Impala, but not one that the Irish kids recognized as belonging to any of them. It rolled slowly east down Root Street on the northern edge of Boyce Field. It moved past some of the parked cars, close enough for some to see into the passenger's open window. One girl near a parked car instantly recognized the teen sitting there as he went by just feet away; she had known him since grade school. "Hi, Horse," she said, using his nickname as the car slowly moved by.

The Chevrolet came to a stop at the corner of Root and Lowe, at the park's northeast corner, and the teens inside began shouting insults.

The Irish kids in the park began to shout back, and some of them acted as if they were going to head for the car. Then suddenly, some did. A group of teenagers charged, at least one of them with a bat in hand.

John Hughes was among them. Hughes heading directly into a confrontation like this was startling even to some of his friends. One saw Hughes bolt in the car's direction, recognizing his jean jacket and yellow shirt out of the corner of his eye, and was so surprised that he joined Hughes in the rush almost without thinking.

The group did not have far to sprint. Maybe twenty or thirty feet, and they covered the ground quickly. Hughes was nearly six feet tall and a star cornerback on the football team. His athleticism put him at the front of the group almost instantly.

The streets were dark, and the car sat directly under a streetlight, the glare obscuring most of the interior of the car in blackness. But those charging could see the teen in the passenger seat. And they could see when he leaned down toward his feet under the dashboard. And they could see whoever was in the driver's seat raise an object over the passenger's back.

One of the charging boys caught its shape. It was a chrome, long-barreled pistol.

One of the first teens to get near the car saw it and tried in vain to stop and run back. His feet hit loose asphalt on the street as he reached the Chevy, and they slipped out from under him. He had been running so hard his momentum carried him forward, and his legs slammed into the rear tire of the car as he skidded.

Hughes had been running almost directly toward the passenger's window. He may have seen the gun as well. He began to try to turn away to his right at the last instant.

There was a flash and a shot.

The bullet flew from the window and into the left side of Hughes's chest, spinning him. He collapsed where he was struck.

Screams of panic rang out. Teenagers were suddenly running everywhere, not knowing what had happened.

The green car accelerated away into the darkness, with Irish kids behind it, yelling. The teen who had slid into the back of the car hurled a bat as the Chevy pulled away, possibly striking it near a taillight.

John's friends immediately came to his side, but his blue eyes were already fading. There was blood coming from his mouth. A dark line of it pooled red under his yellow shirt. Someone tucked a jacket under the red hair of his head as a pillow. "Keep him warm!" someone shouted, as kids began removing their jackets and draping them on top of John. A few ran to nearby houses for help, while one darted into the darkness in a direction where he knew there was a firehouse.

Minutes passed like hours. Where there had been screaming, a stunned silence settled in. "What happened?" teens asked each other. "Who was that?" They looked down at their friend John in disbelief.

Finally, the police appeared. They began asking questions about who had seen what. The fight earlier in the night was mentioned, and police had a good description of the car. Cops who worked the district were aware of which kids were trouble. They had broken up these fights many times before. Pick up the right kid from the Italian side of Pershing and surely the case would crack right open, some officers immediately thought. In fact, a group of teens from Bridgeport were stopped a short time later in the area of the park in a different car, apparently as they came to check what was going on. Some officers expected this would be a quick solve.

John Hughes, meanwhile, had been taken to Mercy Hospital at Michigan Avenue and Twenty-Fifth Street. But he would not be saved. A Dr. Boyd pronounced him dead at 1:20 AM on May 15, 1976.

A tall, good-looking football player and member of the student council, Hughes was supposed to be heading into his senior year, expecting to be student body president the next fall. He had college on his mind. He was going places. Many of John's friends instantly thought of his mother. He was her seventh child, and in some ways the pride of the Hughes family. How could he be the victim of a crime like this?

2

THE FRIEND

Larry Raddatz parked in a small lot in the shadow of a Stevenson Expressway overpass and walked across the street to a Bridgeport staple, Ricobene's, which has been serving its famous breaded steak sandwiches to the neighborhood since World War II.

Raddatz had picked the spot, maybe for some comfort as he reached back through the decades to think about a teenage friend he once knew very well.

He had a somewhat gruff demeanor and a voice with a hint of gravel. He was of Irish and German heritage but, growing up in Canaryville, had leaned toward identification with his Irish roots. And like many men from Irish families, his tough exterior belied a likeable and disarming sensitivity. He looked down at his lunch. He was watching his diet, but every once in a while this was OK.

"Happy-go-lucky. Johnny was always smiling, always laughing. I met him . . ." Raddatz reminisced on that day in 2019, before pausing. "I don't want this to be about me."

It was a phrase repeated in Canaryville and Bridgeport by many of those who had agreed to talk about one of the most painful nights of their lives, a night they had carried with them for decades since. Raddatz was definitely one of those. The trauma of what he had seen was barely below the surface, even more than forty years later. Those who had taken his friend, and those in the city who had done nothing about it, "they can burn in hell," he said, with tears welling in his eyes.

Raddatz had been friends with a guy named John Russell since childhood, and it was Russell who first started hanging around with Hughes. Another of their group was David Gilmartin, John Hughes's cousin, furthering the connection.

Raddatz was two years ahead of Hughes in school. "It was like, *So what. He's big*," Raddatz remembered with a laugh. Hughes was also the same age as Raddatz's younger sister Kathy. "In the neighborhood you know everybody."

Like many kids at that age, Raddatz recalled their time together as doing "a lot of nothing," which meant hanging out at the park and playing sports. It was a tight group—Raddatz, Russell, Hughes, and Gilmartin. Raddatz remembered times they would all drive to the lakefront together with the windows down, Deep Purple's "Smoke on the Water" blasting from the stereo.

Being friends with John was easy. He wasn't quick to get angry or all about himself. He was funny but not distractingly so. He wasn't a class clown and didn't try to pick on kids weaker than him. But he did tend to bring girls around, and he may have shone brightest on the athletic field. He was left-handed and seemed to move fast and with ease while others had to push themselves harder to keep up.

There was always pickup basketball and football to be played. And on some weekends as they grew older, the group would trek together to parties or to another friend's family's place in Michigan for quick warm-weather trips.

"How do you describe any of your friends? You just like being around them," Raddatz said. "Johnny attracted people."

Not everyone in the friend group even went to the same high school, but it didn't matter. Raddatz went to Leo, while Hughes went to De La Salle. Nights and weekends and hours spent at Boyce Field made the real social network. The park was a mecca.

And they had other things in common, like the feud. The Italians and the Irish. Bridgeport and Canaryville. Oil and water. It went back as far as anyone could recall. It was the same with their fathers and in prior generations. Raddatz was among those who didn't even really know why it had started or kept going. The groups just never got along in a city that tended to divide itself up by ethnicity and faction, block by block.

Every kid had a story about the other side. Raddatz was a runner, and in college he had a job at Mercy Hospital. He tended to run there and back home to stay in shape. One day as he cruised along a city street, a car full of Italian kids yelled at him, and one leaned out a window and punched him in the back as they passed, he said.

Fights could start for seemingly no reason. There was a Boys & Girls Club near Thirty-Fifth Street where kids would sometimes congregate, but the Irish kids were careful. "If you had a Canaryville shirt on you'd turn it inside out," Raddatz said, "if you didn't want to get jumped by more guys than you had with you."

That said, Raddatz never recalled Hughes getting in a fight, partly because he just wasn't that way and partly because of his size. The friends weren't really brawlers. Russell was the outgoing class president and Hughes was expected to take over in his senior year.

At the time, Raddatz was the only one with access to a car. It was his parents' 1969 Chrysler New Yorker, and the four friends spent a lot of time driving around in it. Often they would stop at each other's houses, but ultimately they were usually headed to the park. They had girls on their minds and knew girls would be hanging out there with the rest of their friends. They'd flirt and play volleyball. "We used to joke you didn't miss anything if you went out there, but if you didn't go out, that's when everything happened," Raddatz said.

Even when Raddatz graduated high school first, he was nearby at Saint Xavier University, so he would hang out with the same friends on weekends and take in a football game. Hughes had been a starter as a junior, and there was talk he could even play in college. Raddatz was still plugged in to the social circle and still found himself out on weekend nights with his usual group of friends at Boyce Field.

More than forty years later, it was clear how close their friendship had been. The old joking and good-natured rivalry would flash. "John was the best, or one of the best," Raddatz said, laughing. "Maybe one of the best. If I say he was the best it'll be fifty fucking guys calling arguing about who was the best. Let's not say that."

As far as the feud, he remembered May 1976 being no different from normal. There was no more fighting than usual. No one had been looking for trouble as the school year wound down. But if it happened, any of their friends would fight their way out of it. No one would back down, even if they were outnumbered. It was better to take a beating than look soft.

Word had gotten out about the house party in Bridgeport, and kids from both neighborhoods had flocked there. Raddatz and his friends were like moths to the flame, knowing there would be girls and beer and music. But they hadn't been there long when they could tell it wasn't going to be a good place to be. There was bad energy, and the two typical groups were at each other fairly quickly.

There had been other fights at parties where two dozen kids on either side of the feud had wound up rolling around in the street fighting, so the friends left almost as soon as they arrived. They piled back into Raddatz's car and circled back to home base, the park, where they heard there had been more pushing and shoving at the party after they left.

They stood around drinking and talking, before other friends arrived and reported there had been a much larger fight after the party. A group of Italian kids had followed some of their pals on Halsted, and a brawl had ensued.

Some of the guys quickly decided to go back to that area and try to find their longtime foes. There were rumors of other possible fights in other places. John Hughes, Raddatz, and some of their friends jumped back into Raddatz's car as if they were going to join those looking to scrap with the Italians again. But secretly Raddatz didn't want to ruin their night with another fight. He was perfectly happy to stay in the park and have fun. He knew his car wouldn't turn over if he tried to start it after slipping it into neutral, so that's exactly what he did. "My car didn't start because I didn't want it to start," he remembered. "I didn't want to go back and fight."

If there had been a fight in the park, they would have stuck around—those were the unofficial rules of their neighborhood—but Raddatz didn't feel obligated to go looking for trouble. Instead they got to stay at the park drinking beer. Several of his friends stood around his car a few dozen feet from the corner of Root and Lowe.

Not getting his car to start was a simple thing. And at the time, Raddatz thought he was continuing their night of fun and keeping everyone out of harm's way for a time. That would change. And it would become a twist of fate that would stick with Raddatz. Sitting in Ricobene's so many years later, he folded his hands and looked toward the ceiling as he remembered it. "I always felt kind of bad. That I did the thing with the car," he said. "I always . . . It made me feel weak. That I didn't want to go and fight. Would we have been there? I don't know."

It wasn't long until the green Chevrolet slipped toward the park in the darkness. Raddatz could still see it in his mind's eye. The car pulled up under a streetlight and sat there for what seemed like a long time, but it was probably just a few moments. The years have stretched the memory. What unfolded quickly at the time now feels movie-length for those who witnessed it.

Someone in their group noticed the car. There were shouts, both from the Chevy and from Irish kids in the dark of the park. Teens milled around a brick field house near the corner of the park. Some had bats, and it seemed likely that the fight Raddatz had been interested in avoiding was coming to them.

It was hard to fully hear the shouts coming from the car. But there were certainly curses. And suddenly, something unusual happened. Out of the corner of his eye, Raddatz saw the normally mild-mannered John Hughes and some others from his friend group make a break for the corner. John was sprinting for the car, in his full athletic run. And almost without thinking, Raddatz joined in.

"I saw him. I saw Johnny run that way," Raddatz said, recalling his surprise. But it was quickly overcome by wanting to support his friends. "I remember Johnny running and me running toward the car." Even in the dark, they covered the distance quickly, until John was just several feet from the car and Raddatz was trailing just a few feet behind.

Almost over John's shoulder, through the car's open window, Raddatz saw a flash of a face that he knew. It was a teen named NICK COSTELLO. In a fraction of a second, Raddatz's brain made the connection. They hadn't spoken, but Raddatz knew Costello from the softball leagues that used the parks, even right there at Boyce Field. Costello was a good player and was on a team called Rock Party that played against teams in Canaryville.

Sometimes there would be games under the lights at night. There would be beer there too, and of course tempers could flare. A lot of people would show up and there would be a lot of tension and sometimes even fights. Raddatz himself wasn't very good, but he would watch. He had seen Costello play several times, often patrolling first base.

Costello bent in his seat.

Raddatz paused again. At this lunch so many years later, it was clear he was moving on to a memory loop that was never that far from his consciousness. He would describe this again, for a stranger.

In his memory there is no sound. There is no cracking of a gunshot and there is no flash. There is no gun, for that matter. There is Costello moving out of the way for someone behind him in the driver's seat. And there is his friend John spinning in front of him as if an unknown force struck him and knocked him sideways.

"I saw him twirl around and fall," Raddatz said. One of the people carrying a bat threw it, and it cartwheeled toward the back of the fleeing car.

In the chaos that followed, Raddatz leaned over his friend, who was now on his back in the street. Kids were screaming and running, but Raddatz's memory is of his friend's face. "There was blood coming out of his mouth," Raddatz said.

He paused again, for longer this time. In a full restaurant, the pause was long enough that other sounds invaded the conversation. Nearby a table full of children yelled and laughed together. Raddatz overcame the welling emotion of retelling his story. The image remains imprinted in his mind, a horror that will always remain. "I'm sixty-two and I haven't recovered."

The next thing Raddatz knew, he was running.

A few blocks away, he knew there was a fire station. His feet were moving in the dark as fast as they would carry him. He was not about to wait for someone in the park to knock on the door of a house across the street and ask to use the phone. Running was all he could think to do. He ran to the other side of the park past Union, and a block past that to Emerald. A block after that was

Halsted and the fire station. He pounded on the door and told the first person he saw that his friend had been shot in the park.

With that short mission accomplished, the rest of the night fell into a blur. He didn't remember what the firefighter said to him, or how he got back to the park. The next clear image in his mind is the glaring lights inside nearby Mercy Hospital, where Hughes was taken in the back of a squadrol wagon.

Word spread among those who were at the hospital. John was dead. The shocking escalation of the evening gave way to a rushing disbelief.

Raddatz soon found himself struggling. The months that followed were filled with anger, and not a small amount of alcohol, as he tried to come to grips with what had happened. He was filled with sadness, especially at times when he would see John's parents again. The friend group had always been at each other's houses, not doing much but doing it together. Hanging out after school had often carried into the dinner hour, and whichever house they were in, they were all typically welcome for dinner.

He had often had dinner with John and his family, as John's mother moved around the table serving them. "Thank you, Mrs. Hughes," he would say. Now he saw this woman crushed. He saw her weeping at her son's wake and funeral, the vision of it seared into his mind.

There was talk in the early days that the police would quickly move to figure out what had happened. There had been witnesses—after all, the groups had been fighting all night.

Within days, Raddatz was at the police district building on Lowe, viewing a live lineup. Costello was in it, standing right in front of him, he recalled. Raddatz recognized him instantly and said so to the police officers in the room with him. Names of others in the car—even the name of the shooter—were in the air all over the neighborhoods. No one believed this would be a tough crime to solve.

Weeks later, Raddatz was summoned to the main criminal courthouse at Twenty-Sixth and California. But, much to his puzzlement, he was sent home without testifying.

For years, Raddatz blamed himself. Even though he had told police what he saw, he thought he could have done more. He had been just feet away and couldn't see into the dark car past Costello to who was holding the gun. "You feel guilty because you couldn't say, 'I saw that guy. That's who did it,'" Raddatz said, rapping his fingers on the table. "You feel terrible about that, because—*I was there.*"

What did not cross his mind—or enter his friends' thoughts either—was serious revenge. They were typical teens, and none of them had a gun or much of a clue how to get one. It just wasn't something they would have been capable of doing. Beating someone up was one thing; shooting someone in retaliation was another. Raddatz's thoughts were mostly of his friend, the one who should have gone to college and had a family of his own. He was going to be class president and maybe follow an older brother into accounting—or even do something none of them had contemplated yet. All of that was cut short. Raddatz was instead left to marvel at the biggest wake he had ever seen, with hundreds of cars in procession.

John Hughes was big, but he wasn't a bully. He was fun-loving but wouldn't back down if someone challenged him. He was simply a great friend, and one that was taken away.

"I've probably thought about this every day. I see it every day," Raddatz said, before pushing himself away from the table and walking back out into the bright light of a Chicago summer. "It's true. We've lived with this our entire lives."

3

A VISIT WITH THE FBI

I n October 2005, John Furmanek found himself in an unusual place, especially for him.

He was a cop's cop, CPD through and through, and from the school where the FBI wasn't necessarily your friend. The Bureau's agents weren't the real police to someone like Furmanek. They had the snappy suits and the ability to walk into anyone's case and take it over, which they sometimes did. They weren't regular guys from Chicago with deep roots in the culture of law enforcement and connections in city neighborhoods. They were much more likely to be former accountants from Virginia who carried themselves with an air of superiority and butted in where they weren't necessarily wanted.

That included sometimes investigating Chicago police officers themselves, handling police corruption cases and forcing officers to give up information on others. So talking to FBI agents usually meant something wasn't going well for you. Or, at the very least, that some of the department's dirty laundry was about to be aired. That definitely wasn't Furmanek's style. To him, in-house problems should remain in-house problems. The department should police itself, and individual officers should watch each other's backs and hold each other accountable, he believed. Nobody needed the FBI or anyone else getting into department business.

Yet there Furmanek was, walking into an office building a few blocks from the Dirksen US Courthouse in Chicago's Loop. It was the kind of unmarked building where federal authorities sometimes held sensitive interviews like the one Furmanek was about to sit down for. This was a Chicago officer talking to agents and a federal prosecutor who typically handled cases against the local Mafia—the infamous Chicago Outfit, a syndicate with direct lines to the organization of Al Capone. Better to meet away from the courthouse, where there was no chance of someone recognizing Furmanek in an elevator and wondering why he was there.

Furmanek was taking this step because he needed to get some things off his chest from nearly thirty years earlier, things that were clearly bothering him. When John Hughes was killed in 1976, Furmanek was a fairly new tactical officer, and he had assisted in the investigation, such as it was.

After he arrived at the courthouse, Furmanek spoke to two FBI agents, a prosecutor from the Cook County state's attorney's office, and Assistant US Attorney John Scully. Less than two years later, Scully would be one of the prosecutors to bring the sweeping conspiracy case known as Family Secrets against top Chicago mob figures, giving several of them life sentences and closing the books on a collection of homicides.

In fact, it was information related to the Outfit that the agents and prosecutors were looking for when they spoke to Furmanek that day. They logged their report on what Furmanek said under their case on the murder of mob hit man and bookie Ronnie Jarrett, who had been gunned down six years earlier, the first gangland slaying of its kind in several years in Chicago when it happened. Jarrett had been part of the gambling organization of the Twenty-Sixth Street or Chinatown street crew of the Chicago Outfit, and eventually met his demise in an apparent dispute with higher-ups including Johnny "Apes" Monteleone. When Jarrett ended a stint in federal prison, he had essentially started his own bookmaking circle, and it was unclear whether he was paying street tax to the Outfit. Just two days before Christmas in 1999, Jarrett was leaving his family home in Bridgeport near Thirtieth and Lowe, just a few blocks east of McGuane Park, when someone ambushed him and shot him several times. Jarrett had been on his way out to attend a funeral, not knowing he was on a direct path to his own.

The Jarrett killing was still officially unsolved, though it was clear from the federal report on the Furmanek interview that authorities had certain suspects they were looking to link to the murder or other crimes. Their case title made it clear it was an investigation of players in what had been the Chicago Outfit wing run by the late Frank "Skids" Caruso, of which Jarrett had been a part. Also listed in the heading was a man named Rocco "Rocky" LaMantia, the son of a longtime mob figure named Joseph "Shorty" LaMantia.

When Furmanek appeared, federal investigators and Cook County prosecutors already had collected information indicating that Rocky LaMantia was a key suspect in another killing: that of John Hughes. In fact, it indicated that he had been linked to Hughes's murder by some in the early weeks after the shooting. Furmanek did not bring them that information, but he had other curiosities to share about the way the Hughes case was handled, things that had stayed with him to that day. As a police officer, he had been most bothered by the police work in the Hughes case.

And so he began describing what had happened. For starters, Furmanek told them, he and other police officers working the case had been instructed from the start of their efforts to produce only "information" reports as they worked, and not full case reports. That difference meant the reports would not be routed to any file with an actual case number, making them harder to track, if they were saved at all. Furthermore, their reports were not to be stored anywhere or submitted up the usual chain of command. Everything was to be given directly to a commander by the name of John Haberkorn, who led the Ninth District at the time.

Typically, Furmanek's reports would go to a desk sergeant and eventually to the detectives who oversaw a particular investigation. But that never happened in the Hughes case, Furmanek told the FBI agents and prosecutors. In fact, none of his reports were given to the detectives, he said, and he knew many had wound up being destroyed.

Haberkorn was a Bridgeport native who started with the department in 1947. Mayor Richard J. Daley had personally asked that Haberkorn be assigned to the district, which had its headquarters building just a few houses away from the Daley home on Lowe. Unbeknownst to Furmanek on the day of the interview, an FBI file on Haberkorn already existed. In fact, the Haberkorn FBI file had been opened not long after Haberkorn began inserting himself into the Hughes probe.

Furmanek continued. Hughes had been shot in the early morning hours of Saturday, May 15, 1976. And the following Monday, when Furmanek arrived at the Ninth District, a desk sergeant told him he was being asked to report right away to a local restaurant.

It was called the Coral Key, and it sat on South Lowe, not far from the police district building. Of course, Furmanek went, and he wound up in what amounted to an off-the-books briefing, he said. He was ushered to the basement, where he found Sam Cuomo, a cop who went by "David" and ran the restaurant, who Furmanek knew also was assigned as a sergeant-at-arms to the city council; Furmanek's partner Ed Gallagher; and John "Jack" Townsend, a clouted supervisor who had risen from being the chief of security for Mayor Richard J. Daley. Townsend would continue to rise through the ranks to deputy chief of detectives and later to first deputy superintendent of the entire department. There was also a fourth man there whom Furmanek did not know—and who was not introduced to him—and a woman with the last name of Mestrovic, who worked as a waitress at the Coral Key and was counting money in the basement. It's unclear whether those who had summoned Furmanek there knew that Mestrovic had her own unlikely connection to the Hughes case or if she was there completely by chance as an employee who was all but invisible to the officers.

It was also unclear just how stunned Furmanek was by this scene, as the FBI agents did not include anything he might have said about his reaction in the write-up they produced after interviewing him. Townsend's presence at such an odd meeting might have been especially jarring. He was a right-hand man of sorts to the mayor, and everyone knew it. Townsend was himself a lifelong Bridgeport resident with deep connections there.

It was clear, however, what the purpose of the meeting was. Townsend, Cuomo, and the unknown man wanted Furmanek and Gallagher to share their progress on the Hughes murder. They wanted details. And Townsend especially wanted to know any information Furmanek had related to a Nick Costello.

Furmanek told the FBI he had learned the teen, Costello, was Townsend's "nephew," but apparently offered no more details. Or at least the FBI hadn't recorded them.

A few days after the meeting at the restaurant, when Furmanek went to pick Costello up at home to put him in a lineup, he got another surprise. Nick Costello's father answered the door, and Furmanek was stunned to realize he was the unknown fourth man who had been at the Coral Key getting information on the investigation. He was a lieutenant in the Chicago Fire Department. Having a direct relative of a suspect connected to a homicide investigation secretly getting information about the department's progress on the case—with police supervisors present, no less—would certainly have been highly irregular. But again, the FBI agents

Furmanek spoke to in 2005 kept to the basics in their reports and didn't include his reflections on the unfolding events.

The unusual interest in Nick Costello wasn't over. When Furmanek and Gallagher brought the teen in for the lineup at the Ninth District, the brass was all over it again. Townsend and Haberkorn both were present at the station, Furmanek recalled, as was Joseph Curtin, a lieutenant who later became a commander. Two assistant state's attorneys also were present, one of them a key supervisor.

The group watched as an eyewitness to the killing viewed the young men in the lineup. She was Mary Mestrovic, a friend of Hughes who was in the park at the time of the shooting—and was the daughter of the waitress who happened to be in the basement of the Coral Key. She had been standing near the street when the green Chevrolet slowly rolled by, and she had recognized Costello immediately. It wasn't hard. She had gone to grade school with him. She was close enough to speak to him as the car passed, and his window was rolled down. "Hi, Horse," she had said, using his nickname. She told the police Costello was there in the lineup and that he had been in the passenger seat as Hughes was shot, but it wouldn't be recorded that way.

Townsend, Haberkorn, and Curtin went off by themselves, Furmanek told the agents and prosecutors. And within ten minutes of Mary making a positive identification, there was a phone call. Furmanek told the FBI he learned it was a call from the mayor himself. The case wouldn't be progressing, at least that day. Nick Costello walked out of the police station.

For the FBI agents investigating the Jarrett hit, the information Furmanek brought them had no intelligence value in their Outfit case. Furmanek's recollections were recorded on little more than two pages of their file. It's unclear whether the name Nick Costello even meant anything to them or what they thought about the murder of a teenager near four decades earlier.

The name may have meant something to the Cook County prosecutor who was in the Furmanek meeting, however. The state's attorney's office had failed to bring any charges in the Hughes case in the immediate years after his death, but some in the office had picked the case up again in 2000, when a special prosecutors group reviewed it.

An assistant state's attorney named Linas Kelecius was among them. He was part of a cold-case team, and in 2000 he was assigned to the organized crime unit of his office. Even then efforts were being made to link the killing of John Hughes to at least one person with connections to Chicago organized crime.

Kelecius was a veteran prosecutor who, in 2002, would try a case even older than the Hughes murder. Kelecius earned a conviction against Kenneth Hansen, a horseman accused of bludgeoning and strangling John Schuessler, thirteen; his brother Anton, eleven; and their fourteen-year-old friend Robert Peterson at a Northwest Side stable. Their naked bodies had been found on a horse path in a forest preserve in 1955. Hansen was found to have kidnapped, molested, and killed the boys in the infamous case, one that many felt had stripped 1950s Chicago of some of its innocence. Clearly the office was comfortable with bringing a murder case to a jury after decades had passed, and was aiming to do it in the Hughes case.

"Good morning, ladies and gentlemen," Kelecius said to a group of grand jurors at Chicago's main criminal courthouse that day in 2000. "We are not seeking an indictment at this time. We are seeking the testimony at this time of [this witness] regarding a . . . 'John Doe' murder investigation, the murder occurring on May 15 of 1976 at about 1:15 in the morning in the Bridgeport neighborhood of Chicago at Root and Lowe."

Bringing testimony without seeking an indictment meant that the office didn't have the goods to immediately charge anyone or to ask that particular grand jury for a true bill. But the office did often use grand juries as an investigative tool and as a way to lock in testimony during investigations that could be lengthy or in which a witness might be at risk. It was a safeguard of sorts. If a witness died and prosecutors wound up charging their target, they would have a way to read into the record that witness's account at trial. Defense lawyers would protest not getting an opportunity for a cross-examination, but judges often allowed the maneuver anyway.

The witness in question testified that she was thirty-nine that day and that she was divorced from a man named Nick Costello. They had separated fifteen years earlier.

As Kelecius began his line of questioning, he put one thing on the table. He asked whether the witness might be related to Hughes, the victim. And in an answer that perhaps highlighted the interwoven nature of family relationships and connections in Bridgeport, she said that she was. John Hughes was the cousin of her aunt.

That's part of the reason the witness said she wound up having conversations about the shooting with Costello while they were together. There had been a few talks, she said, and she definitely remembered the first one. It had been a few weeks after they started dating, around, say, May 1980, she told Kelecius.

"Can you tell us why you asked about the murder of John Hughes?" Kelecius asked.

"Because when I told my family who I was dating, my mother told my grandmother, my grandmother told my aunt, and my aunt said that he was implicated in the murder of her cousin. So my mother said that to me. So, of course, I had asked him," the witness said. Specifically, she asked Costello whether he had anything to do with it.

"He said, 'No, I was accused of it by a girl that said she seen me pull the trigger and shoot the gun out of a car, and I didn't do it.

And I've suffered and my family has suffered because I have been accused of it,'" she recalled.

It was not certain whether Costello was referring specifically to Mary Mestrovic in the conversation the witness described, though it was probable. Mestrovic was a key eyewitness by all accounts. But she had never told authorities that Costello was the shooter, only that she had seen him in the passenger seat of the car from which the fatal shot was fired. He was either purposefully inflating the Mestrovic account to better his denial or wasn't clear on what Mestrovic had said about him.

A savvy defense lawyer might have eventually used the couple's divorce to suggest the woman Kelecius was questioning before the grand jury was trying to get her ex-husband in trouble as some sort of revenge, but there was also no sign of her exaggerating what she said next.

"Did he tell you who he was with at the time that John Hughes was killed?" Kelecius asked.

"He said he was with his friends, two friends that he did mention, yes, names that I recall he mentioned," the woman said.

One was a teen named PAUL FERRARO, the witness told Kelecius and the grand jury, and the other was Rocco LaMantia.

"Did he tell you where he was with Paul Ferraro and Rocco LaMantia at that time, the time when John Hughes was killed?" Kelecius asked.

"They were just out," she answered. "They were out driving around, I guess."

"Riding around in what?"

"In a car."

She described Costello as being sad about the topic when it would come up. He would say he had been through a lot and not answer questions about it. "He went through a lot of pain and anguish and he felt bad about everything that happened," she said.

Kelecius asked next about Costello's friendships with the two teens he had mentioned to her. One, Ferraro, had stayed his friend. In fact, Ferraro had been invited to the couple's wedding. But her then husband's relationship with LaMantia had cooled.

"Was there any reason why Mr. LaMantia was not his friend during Mr. Costello's relationship with you?" Kelecius asked.

Yes, came the answer.

Could she tell the grand jury what it was?

"He murdered my first cousin," the witness said.

"Who was your first cousin?"

"Martha DiCaro."

LaMantia was dating DiCaro at the time, the witness said. He had been charged with the murder but ultimately acquitted. Kelecius asked why that was, and the witness said she could offer an opinion: "Well, that [LaMantia] had enough money to get in front of the right judge and get a not guilty verdict."

"Do you remember who the judge was?" Kelecius asked.

"Maloney," she answered.

And what wound up happening to Maloney? "He was sentenced, I believe, to jail, for taking bribes for fixing murder trials," she said.

Kelecius asked if the witness had spoken to anyone in the last days or weeks about what she had just testified to. She said detectives had knocked on her door about a week earlier. She had told her mother and a few girlfriends that she had been approached.

Her testimony was winding down. She clearly had been called to lock in her exchange with her former husband as the case was being recirculated once again.

One grand juror had a question: Did Costello ever say he knew John Hughes?

He knew of him, the witness said. They weren't friends but knew each other because they were in the same age group. She said she never got any details from her ex-husband about what had led up to Hughes being killed. She only heard from relatives what they thought had led up to it.

"Were you reluctant to talk about the John Hughes murder with him after having conversed about it in the beginning of your relationship?" Kelecius asked as he wrapped up the session.

The witness said yes, she was.

And why was that? "Because it upset him. He became very saddened and despondent," she answered. "He didn't want to talk about it. That was part of his life that he wanted to forget about."

4

A CASE TO LOOK INTO

When John Hughes was killed, Jim Sherlock was in sixth grade at St. Adrian Grammar School near Marquette Park in Chicago. St. Adrian was the local Catholic church, most famous perhaps for its 7 PM mass on Sunday evenings, the one parents could still get to if they had too much fun on Saturday night.

As far back as he remembered, Sherlock had wanted to be a Chicago police officer. It was in his blood. His grandfather and great-grandfather had both been cops. He still had a photo of his great-grandfather in an old Chicago park police uniform with an old-time hat. Another big guy from Ireland—Limerick, to be specific.

But it was his grandfather in whose steps he felt he was following the closest. His name was also Jim Sherlock, and he too was an officer and detective in some of the city's toughest areas. He had lied about his age to get on the department in the first place. "How old do I have to be?" that Jim Sherlock had asked. He got an answer and replied, "Well, that's how old I am."

He took a break from policing to fight in WWII as a tank commander in Africa and then returned and worked a long police career until 1969, the year after Chicago and its department were rocked by the protests and response at the 1968 Democratic National Convention. The nation had watched as Chicago cops in their light-blue riot helmets had bludgeoned young protesters at Mayor Richard J. Daley's direction.

Sherlock's father had gone to the police academy but took a different career path. Both of Sherlock's sons, however, Jack and Jim Sherlock IV, would also join the department.

Sherlock would think of his grandfather on nights he found himself in Woodlawn, one of the spots the elder Sherlock had worked. The neighborhood was home to Mount Carmel High School, another all-boys school that all four Jim Sherlocks had graduated from.

Things moved quickly for Sherlock after he left the school, headed for Purdue University in Indiana. His girlfriend became pregnant at eighteen, and they married. She stayed home while he went to Purdue for a criminology degree, knowing he was headed for CPD. He took and passed the department's qualifying exam in 1984, but it would take five years for him to get on the job.

In the meantime, he waited while working for the Cook County sheriff's office. And after finally fulfilling his dream of becoming a police officer in Chicago, he was sent straight to Englewood, where he made friends and took to the job quickly.

Over his thirty-year career, Sherlock would prove to have a knack for being in the orbit of major events in the department's history, including some of its great tragedies. The pattern started early.

His best friend working for Cook County was a fellow recruit named John Knight. The two had worked together whenever they could after both made it to CPD and finished their training. Eventually Sherlock went to gangs, and Knight went to Morgan Park, the Twenty-Second District.

When Sherlock, now a detective, arrived for work on January 9, 1999, he noticed things seemed a little quieter than normal. As he sat down at his desk, someone said solemnly, "I guess you didn't hear the news. John was killed."

"John who?" Sherlock answered, before the information sank in. Suddenly the room was noisy again as he tried to quickly gather what had happened.

Knight had gone to work as usual in the Twenty-Second District, sniffing out crime as a tactical officer in an undercover car with a partner. On that snowy day, he was planning to leave early to make it to a wedding. He had barely started the shift when he and his partner noticed a parked car with its trunk lock punched out and two men slumping inside as if they didn't want to be seen.

The unmarked squad approached, and the suspicious car lurched forward, as quickly as it could considering the slick streets. It was not a long chase. The snow proved too slippery for a getaway, and the car crashed in the intersection of Ninety-Ninth and Parnell near the Dan Ryan Expressway. Both occupants jumped out, but one of them, a man named James Scott, had drugs on him and had no intention of being arrested. Before the officers could get out of their car, Scott turned and pulled out a 9mm handgun with a laser sight and fired. Knight's partner returned fire and hit Scott, who was arrested after responding officers followed a trail of blood in the snow. He was later convicted by a jury.

Knight had been struck twice in the head. He was thirty-eight and left a wife and three children. It was a death that affected Sherlock deeply, even two decades later as he recalled his friend. He often called it his single worst day on the job.

Even his years working on a strike force unit in the mid-1990s hadn't produced a tragedy of that magnitude. Sherlock had been a young buck on one of the most aggressive parts of CPD, with just a few years as a cop. Most of the guys working with him had been on for ten or fifteen years and were much more experienced. They worked stopping cars and making arrests, looking for guns and drugs.

It was there that Sherlock got to know another member of this rock 'n' roll police crew, an officer by the name of Jerome Finnigan. To Sherlock then, Finnigan was just another young, aggressive cop. But he was an officer who would take a drastic turn, going on to claim an infamous place in CPD history and eventually sparking the end of what came to be called the special operations section.

In a group like SOS, tactical officers were given nearly free rein to work informants and drug networks to locate narcotics and guns on the street—the kind of job that often put large amounts of cash and drugs at their fingertips, with little supervision. The only accounting would take place when it came time to inventory what they had seized, giving crooked officers the chance to skim what they had found or pocket it outright. When something went missing, drug dealers either would not complain, fearing reprisals and chalking it up to the cost of doing business, or would be in a situation in which it was their word against an officer's. Finnigan and his small circle took things even further, crossing into home invasions and theft from regular citizens they came across on the job. They were even accused of robbing and beating a Chicago firefighter.

Complaints and lawsuits from people with little or no criminal record led to much more scrutiny. Authorities started looking and noticed the Finnigan group would often make drug arrests but never show up in court. Then the city settled a 2002 lawsuit filed by a man who contended Finnigan and other cops pulled him from his truck before robbing and threatening him.

Finally, in 2006, Finnigan and several other cops, including an officer named Keith Herrera, were charged as a criminal ring, accused of burglary, aggravated kidnapping, and other crimes. Finnigan, who had previously won an award for valor, had been on the department for seventeen years.

The allegations were spectacular, placing the Finnigan crew in the pantheon of the worst Chicago police officers ever. They were accused of planting drugs on people and forcing them to turn over cash they had in their homes. Often, they targeted immigrants with little ability to defend themselves. In one event, they stopped a man at a gas station and demanded his home address. One officer drove him around while the others went to his house. There they found shopping bags containing more than $450,000, which they would later split up. But the money wasn't drug proceeds, it was the result of a real estate transaction in Mexico, and the victim had proof. The crumbling of the police crew led Cook County prosecutors to drop more than one hundred cases they had worked and charged.

Then, in 2007, federal authorities accused Finnigan of crossing yet another line. They alleged he had tried to take out a hit on a fellow officer who had flipped against him. He and Herrera had discussed hiring someone to do it, but Finnigan didn't know Herrera was wearing a wire for the FBI at the time. The chatter had started with Finnigan telling Herrera that members of a Chicago street gang would take $5,000 to do the killing, which he coded as a "paint job." Finnigan later told investigative reporter and author Hillel Levin in the April 2012 edition of *Playboy* that he called it that in reference to the book *I Heard You Paint Houses*, based on the accounts of Frank Sheeran, who claimed to have bumped off Jimmy Hoffa. Sheeran's story was the basis for the hit movie *The Irishman*.

Finnigan later started to switch off of the idea, telling Hererra, "I'm lookin' for better prices for painting." He wanted an option less risky than the gang members. "Professional painters, dude," Finnigan was recorded saying. He told Herrera he was looking at someone with no connections to him that would not create a trail, a person who "has done a lotta paint jobs."

Finnigan would plead guilty to federal crimes and get twelve years, though he later contended he did not concoct the murder-for-hire plan. Herrera got a light sentence in exchange for his cooperation.

Finnigan was released from prison in 2018 and spoke to Sherlock, who recalled better times with him. They had found money and guns back when they worked together, and taking things for themselves hadn't crossed their minds, at least as far as Sherlock knew. Still coming into his own as a cop, Sherlock had marveled at the way Finnigan moved through the city. If Finnigan was growing too close to some sources at that time, it hadn't stood out to Sherlock.

Once, after the two had stopped working together, Sherlock and another group of officers were working near California and Flournoy in a tough neighborhood. They cuffed someone they had arrested and put him in their car, but one of them forgot they had placed their handheld radio on the car's roof.

"What was that?" one of the cops said as they pulled away, not realizing it was the radio cartwheeling onto the asphalt behind them.

At the station they realized their mistake. It was a loss that might mean a paperwork headache—and that placed a radio in the field that someone could use to monitor police movements. A thought came into Sherlock's mind. *Call Finnigan.*

"Give me half an hour," Finnigan said when Sherlock reached him. That was fine. Sherlock decided to grab a bite to eat.

About forty-five minutes later, there was Finnigan with the radio. "Don't ask me how I got it," he said. Sherlock later learned Finnigan had put the word on the street ordering that the radio be returned. A contact had said the radio would be left under a garbage can at a certain address, and sure enough, that's where it had been found. To Sherlock, Finnigan's methods had been unusual, but never a sign of anything sinister.

Sherlock made detective in 1997, and one of his early tasks was working sting operations on L trains moving in and out of downtown Chicago. Once officers noticed a pattern of theft reports on a given train, they would move in with a small team. Undercover cops would dress in plain clothes and act drunk on the train while wearing a nice watch or leaving cash hanging from a pocket, hoping to lure a thief.

Many officers would work security jobs on the side to make extra money, and Sherlock was no different. One such job had him at a giant bar called the Baja Beach Club, which once sat inside the North Pier building in Streeterville. A fellow officer was walking in one day and asked Sherlock what he might be doing in the next twenty-four hours. There was a security spot if he could show up around the corner at the NBC Tower.

"There's a TV show there called *The Jerry Springer Show,*" his friend told him. Sherlock had never heard of it.

Springer in its early days had been more like a straight-up talk show, like *Donahue* or many others on the airwaves. But its producers were working on a formula that would set the program apart for years to come. They would concoct situations that would push guests who sat with Jerry Springer to their breaking points so punches eventually would be thrown as the crowd went crazy. More often than not the premise of the show was taking apart a love triangle or otherwise exposing a secret affair. The audience came to expect a fracas, and Springer delivered, over the trademark chant of "Jerry! Jerry! Jerry!"

Sherlock assumed when his friend asked him to stop in to work security that he would be guarding the lobby or something. But sure enough, Sherlock found himself in the front row of the studio audience.

His job, he learned, was to let the guests interact physically, but not to a degree where anyone was hurt too badly. Those running the show would prescreen guests for explosive situations, sometimes welcoming them from other states. The green room would be stocked with high-caffeine drinks to make sure everyone was good and wound up. They would keep the would-be combatants separated until they were on stage, boosting the element of surprise.

Sherlock was puzzled at first. How long was he supposed to let them fight? He was a police officer after all. But the instructions never improved. "I want action," a producer would say, "but nobody better get hurt."

The result was the security guards being yelled at one day for jumping on stage too early as they tried to head something off and then another day being yelled at for not interfering sooner after a solid punch was landed. Meanwhile, the audience ate it up.

In one instance, Sherlock found himself trying to separate a groom from his best man, after the best man had revealed to the bride that the groom had cheated on her with a stripper at the bachelor party. The place went up for grabs, and Sherlock had to contend with two young, athletic guys who were legitimately trying to strangle each other. It ended with Sherlock at the bottom of a pile of people with the groom in a headlock.

"What the fuck did you think was going to happen?" Sherlock said into the guy's ear as they struggled. "You're on *The Jerry Springer Show*, man."

All the televised brawling eventually got the show sideways with local politicians, and it wore out its Chicago welcome. Internal struggles over production eventually pushed it to Connecticut, but not before Sherlock got tasked with doing some scouting for Jerry out of state. Producers wanted to put a guy on who claimed to have married and slept with his horse. Sherlock traveled to Joplin, Missouri, to see if it was real, and ended up in a trailer with the man and his love. There were wedding photos.

The double life was a bit of a head trip when Sherlock would leave the set at 4:00 PM and head to Area One to work homicides, but it helped pay the bills. And Sherlock counted Springer and the show's producers as friends for years after the circus left Chicago.

Many of the homicides Sherlock handled were back-and-forth gang killings that have persisted in the city for decades, but a few stood out and made headlines. Among the most high-profile cases he dealt with was the murder of an off-duty cop named Brenda Sexton, who worked as a patrol officer in the Chicago Lawn district after joining the department in 1997. She was killed by her boyfriend, Samuel Lupo Jr., who attacked her with a baseball bat during a fight in August 2000. Lupo bludgeoned Sexton in the head and face, striking her at least nine times and leaving her with fatal injuries that shook even the most hardened detectives.

Lupo fled to Wisconsin, and Sherlock was among the Chicago officers to swarm north of the border. The getaway vehicle had attracted some attention in the vacation town of Lake Delton, being a teal Pontiac Firebird and all. An officer had chased the fugitive Lupo after noticing his conspicuous car, which Lupo abandoned near a strip club named Cruisin' Chubby's.

He fled into the woods. The Chicago media was also in pursuit, and it was a television reporter and a cameraman who found Sexton's 9mm service pistol in some tall grass near Lupo's abandoned Firebird.

Dogs and a helicopter rigged with infrared sensors eventually flushed Lupo out of his hiding place and into custody. He was captured just a mile from where officers including Sherlock had staged their search. The case stuck with Sherlock not only for the terrible killing of a fellow officer but also for what happened next. The law enforcement team members were congratulating each other and having a bite to eat as they shook hands. But as they were saying their goodbyes, the helicopter team that had helped them took off and, in a tragic accident, immediately crashed, killing two Milwaukee County sheriff's officers.

Lupo eventually pleaded guilty and was sentenced to sixty years.

By 2003, Sherlock was starting to work with federal authorities, first assisting the US Marshals group known as the Great Lakes Regional Fugitive Task Force, which did exactly as the name implies. High-stakes fugitives around the region were targeted for arrest, the group traveling far and wide to track down those who needed to be brought in to face their alleged crimes, including many from Chicago.

Sherlock often found himself on roving teams, looking for those who were trying their best to stay hidden or sneak into a new life. Other times the action came to them, like the time a group of kidnappers shot and killed a woman in Atlanta, took another captive, and began heading toward Chicago. They didn't know the woman had managed to hide a phone on her body, and that she had used it to text a friend for help. Authorities began tracking the phone as it pinged from cell tower to cell tower while they headed north. The marshals eventually tracked it all the way to a motel in Zion, Illinois, where they rescued the woman and arrested three men.

As his time with the marshals was winding down, Sherlock began to work with the FBI. He was chosen to assist a violent crimes task force that was investigating a brazen burglary crew linked to the Chicago Outfit. Its members were knocking off big targets, including the stash houses of major drug cartels that were using Chicago as a national distribution center for their product. The crew would go as far as tracking dealers with GPS devices and wearing fake badges during confrontations.

The FBI eventually set up an elaborate sting to catch the crew. Agents created a fake stash house in the Hegewisch neighborhood on Chicago's Southeast Side, and then put the word on the street through cooperating informants that kilos of cocaine were being stored there. The crew took the bait. The FBI was watching, including with a spy plane, as two reputed Chicago Outfit soldiers, Paul Koroluk and Robert Panozzo, moved in. Both were career criminals, with Panozzo linked to noted Outfit boss Joey "the Clown" Lombardo of the Chicago mob's Grand Avenue street crew, who died in 2019.

Agents had leaked the fake tip that two men were working security on the house, and that they would go to lunch each day early in the afternoon. Koroluk and Panozzo had no idea the house had been wired with cameras when they kicked in a door, acting like cops themselves, with Koroluk wearing a silver police star around his neck. The FBI team waited for the pair to grab the packages of drugs before popping out of a nearby garage and taking them into custody. Both eventually took heavy prison terms.

For Sherlock, it was a thrilling later stage of his career. He was considered a top-notch detective, with sharp interviewing skills. And he was affable. The feds liked working with him as much as he liked working with them. In March 2016, the FBI asked Sherlock to assist them on a more permanent basis. He would work with the FBI's CE-6, which stood for "Criminal Enterprise," and specifically a cold-case homicide group. Most officers would go their entire career and never see such a plum assignment, working with some of the best investigators in the country with all the resources of the federal government at their disposal. Sherlock began working each day at the FBI's Chicago headquarters near Roosevelt Road and Ogden Avenue.

To find cases to look at, Sherlock used his considerable network of current and former Chicago police officers—especially the former ones. They had long memories, and many had left some things unfinished. It was a retired commander who suggested, for example, that Sherlock have a look at the mysterious 1984 stabbing death of a City Colleges of Chicago professor who also served as a choir director at a Catholic church on the South Side.

Francis Pellegrini was a social science teacher and the choir director and organist at a church on South Prairie Avenue. And he was a bit of a community figure, a former director of the civic committee that organized Chicago's Columbus Day parade each year. His body was found in the basement of a Bridgeport home he shared with his mother in May 1984. He had been bound and stabbed some twenty times in the head, arms, chest, and back.

There was no forced entry into the apartment on South Parnell Avenue and nothing was out of place, so police immediately put out information that they believed they were looking for an acquaintance or even someone Pellegrini knew well. Among their clues were that neighbors told them Pellegrini's dog was somewhat unfriendly to strangers, and Pellegrini was known to put it in a back room when visitors he didn't know well came by. Instead of finding the dog in that back room, police noted the dog was in the basement with Pellegrini and had sustained a stab wound of its own.

Sherlock learned a young student who knew Pellegrini from the church had confided in the choir director that a priest was abusing him and that Pellegrini supposedly was going to report it. He was attacked and killed before he did.

Sherlock looked into whether the motive was to protect the priest and others that were involved in some type of sex ring—an investigation that quickly started to sound like a plot from a movie thriller, where the cover-up goes all the way to the Vatican. What Sherlock learned was that the Pellegrini killing might be linked to at least two more deaths. The plot Sherlock investigated included the possibility that a suspect in the brutal murder was involved in the same sex ring, and that he had hired three hit men to kill a former roommate who could link him to Pellegrini's slaying. On the way to do the job in the suburbs, the allegation went, the three men had been stopped by a Cook County sheriff's officer, who was then shot and killed. The trio was arrested and later tried and convicted in the officer's killing.

Concerned that he could be informed on and tied to Pellegrini and the botched hit job, the man who hired the group had supposedly hired yet another man to shoot *him* to make it look like he also had been attacked, as opposed to being the mastermind. But that hadn't gone particularly well either, allegedly, as the shooting ruse was a little too convincing and the man died of his wound a few days later.

It was a mess for sure, and it wasn't likely to result in any fresh charges. So Sherlock was considering moving on when that same retired commander called in a message to Sherlock that an FBI assistant wrote down on a piece of paper for him. The message included some information about the Pellegrini case, but on the same slip was a note that there was another cold-case killing Sherlock might consider looking into next. It was a murder from 1976.

Sherlock returned the call not long afterward and asked about it. There was a name: John Hughes. A teenager who had been killed, and nothing had been done.

And there was a word of caution. "When you start looking into this," the retired commander told Sherlock, "buckle up."

5

THE GORMAN FILE

Sherlock walked up the two flights of stairs at an evidence center on the South Side of the city as he had many times before, although on this summer day in 2018, it was with more anticipation than usual.

He was at the records center at Thirty-Ninth and Michigan to see the case file for X-178274. It was the record number for the murder of John Hughes. Sherlock waited as a clerk he was friendly with left to retrieve it.

Typically the file for any unsolved murder case stays at the CPD area handling it, basically forever. But in this instance, Area Three had closed. Most of its paperwork had been moved over to the evidence center, a three-story brick building with rows of block-glass windows to keep it safe. Sherlock knew much of the Hughes file must be there.

He waited. His mind wandered toward what he was about to do. He was essentially going to treat the case as if it were new: find anyone who was still alive to answer questions about what had happened in 1976. Certainly there were people out there who could help him. Now he was working with the FBI. That was different than just talking to another police detective who was showing interest in the case. More than forty years had passed, so some might think the danger in telling him what they knew had gone by the wayside.

But step one would be to digest the complete police file that had started piling up in 1976 and had surely been added to since. Were there signs that things had not been handled properly? Had a detective overlooked a witness then who could assist him now? Who knew how long it would take to pick through all of that paper.

The clerk reemerged. He handed Sherlock a thin manila folder.

"Um, where's the rest of it?" Sherlock asked. "Where are the Bankers Boxes?"

But there were none.

A brazen murder in a public park that had taken a promising teenager from his family, which allegedly had been investigated by teams of detectives for years, and which supposedly involved supervisors and had been reviewed by prosecutors, had yielded only this meager paper trail. What should have been a massive file with notes and transcripts from dozens of interviews had been reduced to a few seemingly random sheets of paper from reports and a couple of photographs.

As the surprise wore off, Sherlock knew how his last months with the Chicago Police Department would be spent. He could have left the records center without the folder and cruised into retirement without taking on the case after all, and no one would have noticed.

Instead, he tucked the envelope under his arm and carried it outside.

Sherlock didn't even drive back to the office before having a look at the file. He was still parked outside the records center when he started sifting through what there was of it—easily under twenty pages total. It began with an evidence report prepared the night Hughes died.

"Homicide," it started. "Root & Lowe." Police had arrived about ten minutes after the shooting. There was very little evidence to collect at the scene. There was no shell casing found from the single shot, meaning either it had been ejected in the interior of the car or the gun used was a revolver.

The only photos taken were of Hughes's ID, his wound, and the scene. One plastic bag of his clothing was logged and listed as going to the lab: a yellow shirt and a blue jacket.

"Above victim fatally shot by unknown persons while victim was standing with a group of his friends at Root and Lowe streets," the report stated plainly. "Offenders were riding in an auto and shot was fired at random at the group. Victim printed at Mercy Hospital and wound noted in left chest area. Scene processed for pertinent evidence with negative results."

Another page in the file was a sheet showing that a lineup had been conducted in the early morning hours the same night Hughes was killed. Nick Costello was in it. He had been stopped along with a carload of teens in a different vehicle that had been near the park in the couple of hours after the shooting. Costello appeared in the lineup in the third position, according to the paperwork.

"No positive identification made by persons viewing," it stated. And accompanying it was a photo of the purported lineup. Costello seemed to be standing a half step in front of the other six teens with him in front of what looked to be a row of lockers. He had a shaggy Jim Morrison–style head of hair and was wearing a bright yellow leather jacket. He would have been hard to miss. According to the file, at least two teens had seen the lineup and not picked out Costello: Hughes's friends Larry Raddatz and John Russell.

Sherlock thought the inclusion of the lineup report was unusual for more than one reason. The most conspicuous one was that CPD protocol was not to make detailed reports or photograph negative lineups. It was as if someone had tried to create a record that Costello had not been identified.

There was another sheet with a handwritten note that said a July 1975 lineup photo had been ordered printed. That was the wrong year, but the photo was not included anyway.

The file, already notably odd, was not improving as Sherlock kept going through it. The next sheet included a photo of a car that CPD apparently looked at in connection with the murder. It had been driven to the Ninth District from a garage on South Emerald because "this auto answers the description of one used in homicide 15 May 76."

It was logged two months after the killing, in July. There it was in a photo. Sherlock held it for a close look. It was sitting on a city street. But there was one big problem. It was blue and had a black vinyl top. No one had given a description of a car that included those colors.

Finally, there was one more sheet in the file on a different car, and this was much more promising. Someone had processed a vehicle later the Saturday of the shooting. It was a green 1972 Chevrolet. Someone had taken three photos of it, but those weren't in the file.

Wow, Sherlock thought, *that's a clue*. Where had this car come from? How did police find it? Who owned it? The officer who processed the car noted that he had arrived to do the job at 6:20 in the evening and was done by 6:50. But, of course, the other pertinent information was not in the report. There was a line available for someone to fill in the location where the Chevy had been found.

"NONE," someone had written.

Sherlock knew that to get his FBI bosses to bite and approve him going forward full throttle in their name, he would need to bring them at least the start of a case. It didn't have to be much. He first needed to convince himself that there was at least a nugget of truth—just enough to pick at and see if another run at the same evidence could support a new investigation. And then he needed to use it to convince the FBI that this would be worth his time.

If he had to reduce the case to one interview, Sherlock knew what that meant. He had one lead to work with. He needed to talk to Mary Mestrovic, who had been in the park and who had been so sure of seeing "Horse" roll by in the Chevrolet. Furmanek had told the FBI about her in 2005, and she was mentioned in the few reports Sherlock had. Maybe there was a reason police and prosecutors had seemingly buried her account. Maybe they had, for some reason, discredited her testimony and hadn't ignored what seemed like a compelling eyewitness account from a frightened teenager who knew what she had seen.

Sherlock was a skilled interviewer. He would be able to tell if she hadn't really seen what she said she did, or if she was mentally unstable and a crummy witness. Talking to Mestrovic was the quickest way to an immediate thumbs-up or thumbs-down ruling on the case. She was in many ways the hinge it would swing on.

Because of his own police background, he still had doubts that respectable police officers could have shoved something like this into a hiding place where it had stayed for decades. Reading the case file, however, Sherlock's instincts told him that Mestrovic had correctly identified Costello. She knew him. Why would she lie? There had to be a reason officers hadn't pursued him. "Something must be wrong with her," he said to himself.

Mestrovic was not hard to find. She was a retired Chicago Public Schools teacher, and she still lived in Bridgeport, where she had been her whole life. He parked outside her simple brick home, almost literally in the shadow of the White Sox ballpark, and walked up the steps.

Mary greeted him at the door, and they went inside to have coffee at the kitchen table. She was unassuming, looking like many women in the neighborhood. She wasn't flashy and was clearly not one to put on airs. She had a quiet personality, and she spoke slowly and steadily. She was also thoughtful, Sherlock noticed, seemingly not wanting to say an unnecessary word. His instant impression was that she wished none of this had come to her. She certainly wasn't seeking attention, and although Sherlock found himself at ease around her, she hadn't been eager to meet with him in the first place.

Almost instantly, even before they got into the meat of the conversation Sherlock wanted to have, a feeling crawled into his stomach as he looked at her. Call it a detective's senses, but Sherlock knew. He had half expected to need to find an excuse to leave after realizing Mestrovic was a crackpot with a bad story. Instead the opposite was happening. The feeling in his gut was not that there was a problem with Mary but that something was very wrong with the police work that had taken place in 1976.

Just talking to her, all his truth detectors went off at once. It was his own voice in his own head. *She's legit.*

In fact, Sherlock quickly realized it was Mestrovic who doubted *him*, not the other way around. She had been trying to do the right thing since day one, and nothing ever came of it. Every few years, another officer or investigator would appear out of the blue and ask her questions yet again, and then disappear just as quickly. To her, Sherlock was just another guy who would look at the Hughes case and go away with hardly a whisper.

That was fair, Sherlock told her. "But I'm not going away," he said. "I'm going to do something. Whatever I can."

He explained to her the issues with bringing someone to justice. It was many decades after the shooting. There was little physical evidence at the time, let alone after so much time had passed. Ultimately, it would be what detectives called a "statement case."

Someone who had been involved in the shooting would have to tell the story of what had happened, and that was an uphill battle for any investigator.

Adding to her credibility, Mestrovic was immediately apologetic for what she didn't remember. There were only so many details she could pull back from a night that had in some ways altered her as a teenager and stolen a measure of peace from her forever. Sherlock was reassuring. In every sense, Mestrovic had been an innocent bystander. She had said hello to Costello from just a few feet away, not knowing she was about to witness a shocking murder. "It wasn't like you were waiting for a shot to be fired," he told her.

And in many ways, that vulnerability only made Mestrovic more believable. She was not going to embellish her memory. And if she had seemingly only memorized a rigid set of facts from forty years earlier, it would have made Sherlock more doubtful of the story. Instead, her thoughts and recollections were organic, and gave Sherlock confidence that he could rely on her.

Even just after the killing, Mestrovic had been reluctant, she remembered. It was her mother who had cajoled her into talking to officers. Hughes had been her friend, and it was the right thing to do. Her mother had been right, she told Sherlock—she had to do it, and from then on she had been as helpful as she could.

And so in her quiet way, she repeated her story to Sherlock. She had been at the party on Throop Street, and recalled the arguing among "the boys" from McGuane Park and their counterparts from Boyce Field, choosing to describe them by the centers of their social world instead of by neighborhood. She had wound up back at Boyce herself after the party became uncomfortable, remembering being there with at least twenty to thirty people. She then walked Sherlock through seeing "Horse" go by in the green car and the shot coming from it moments later.

Within a couple of days, she said, she was picked up from school and taken to the Ninth District police station. An officer named John Haberkorn had been the one to ask her about what happened, she recalled, not knowing his rank but definitely realizing he was a boss. Sherlock knew he was actually the district commander and that him doing the interview at all would have been highly unusual.

Mestrovic specifically remembered viewing two lineups. One had Costello in it. She knew him, and again, had no difficulty pointing him out to police. She was then showed a second lineup, she said, and that one had no one in it whom she recognized. This version of events further troubled Sherlock, who knew the official police record only mentioned a single, negative lineup.

What Mestrovic said next was even more worrisome. After she told police and a top prosecutor what she saw, she had overheard some of them dismissing and mocking her. She had become confused and upset, not really knowing what was going on. One mimicked her voice and accused her of being drunk in the park and made her cry.

As she described what had happened, Sherlock realized he had stopped taking notes. He was dumbfounded and simply listening. What in the world had happened?

Mestrovic said she was still later brought before a grand jury and had told the exact same story. It had been a month later, but she still knew she had seen Costello in the car that had rolled by her, stopped at the corner, and had a gunshot fired from it. Sherlock had no doubt that if a grand jury had heard a teenaged Mary tell them what she saw with the kind of clarity she still had years later, they would have returned a true bill allowing the case to proceed.

But that only joined the list of problems he had found. There was no record anywhere in the files that Mestrovic had testified to a grand jury. No transcript or sheet advising that such an appearance had taken place at all. It had been tossed completely.

He closed his report on the conversation with Mestrovic's own memory corroborating a meeting at the Coral Key. "A short time after the incident at Boyce Park, Mestrovic stated her mother, Rita Mestrovic, who was a waitress at the Coral Key restaurant, witnessed a Chicago police sergeant Dave Cuomo and other unknown Chicago police brass talking with the Bridgeport group who were involved in the Hughes incident," he wrote for his FBI file. "This event took place in a basement room of the restaurant. Metrovic's mother told her that she heard Cuomo telling the boys not to cooperate with police and to stay quiet.

"Investigation continues," Sherlock wrote.

Sherlock wanted to speak as soon as he could to Ellen Hughes Morrissey. She was the sister of John Hughes, and Sherlock wanted to inform her that he and the FBI had taken interest in her brother's death. He wasn't necessarily looking for a blessing, but a strongly negative family reaction might have made him think twice about wading back into a case that was going to be thorny as it was.

The first time they made contact was on the phone. Sherlock told her that the task force he was a part of, CE-6, made up of detectives, agents and prosecutors, would be doing a top-to-bottom review. He logged her response in plain language for his next report. "Morrissey welcomed the news, however, warned there have been investigative attempts in the past by the Chicago Police Department, private investigators, and private attorneys that have been thwarted by unknown individuals," he wrote. "Morrissey stated that she and her family believe corrupt police officers were working in unison with members of organized crime to keep those responsible for the death of her brother out of jail."

Sherlock was quickly starting to agree that could very well be the case. Morrissey told him one private investigator the family hired had returned to their home less than a week after taking on the job. He was so rattled, he took her parents into the backyard, fearing their house could be bugged. He was no longer interested in helping them, he said, and it might be best for them to move on as well.

That was certainly unusual, Sherlock thought. But something else Morrissey said intrigued him more. A man named Jimmy Gorman, who had since died, was a Chicago police officer at the time her brother was shot. He had performed his own sort of shadow investigation years later and had been in contact with members of the Hughes family. Unlike some private investigators, Gorman originally could have had access to paperwork from inside the police department. It was possible that some of Sherlock's missing reports and files might still exist; Gorman could have spirited them out of the records without anyone knowing. It was a lead worth tracking down.

Within a few weeks, Sherlock was talking to Gorman's daughter in West Beverly on the city's far South Side, very near to his own home. Her father had been a policeman in the Ninth District when the shooting took place, but she didn't know why he had gotten so involved seemingly on his own. Gorman had eventually left the department and become a firefighter, and then left that job to finish law school and become an assistant Cook County state's attorney and later go into private practice. He, too, had gone to the FBI with what he knew in 2005, Sherlock learned, possibly later convincing Furmanek to step forward.

Gorman's daughter remembered the Hughes name and, much more important, remembered seeing a file box on the case in the storage area of her father's law office, which she and Sherlock were standing in that day.

Sherlock laughed to himself and shook his head. He had grown up around Seventy-First and Kedzie, in Marquette Park, but had moved to West Beverly more than twenty years earlier, virtually around the corner. When Ellen Hughes had mentioned a Jimmy Gorman who had become a lawyer, something had fired in Sherlock's mind. He knew a lawyer by that name, he thought. That's because Gorman's name was still hanging on a sign outside the office where he was now talking to Gorman's daughter. One of Sherlock's favorite bars, Barney Callaghan's on Western Avenue, was almost next door, so he had walked by this place many times.

"I'll get the file box for you," Gorman's daughter told him. It might take a little digging around, so Sherlock asked her to give him a ring when it turned up.

Except that it didn't. For some reason, the file Gorman's daughter had seen so many times was no longer there, and she couldn't explain it. She was the new senior partner at the firm, so nothing should have been removed or destroyed without her knowledge.

Unbelievable, Sherlock thought. Every time he thought he was getting a break, this case seemed to move ahead of him, staying just out of his grasp.

Pat Bovenizer and John Hughes had almost considered themselves brothers. Their mothers were first cousins, and beyond the relation, they were very good friends. Bovenizer was often in the crew that hung out with Hughes at Boyce Field, though he wasn't present on May 15, 1976. He had always felt a sense of guilt, for some reason, that he wasn't there the night John died. It wasn't like he could have done much about it, but there the guilt was, just the same.

The rumor that Sherlock was looking under rocks for information on the murder came to Bovenizer through neighborhood channels. There was a certain buzz that this time things might be different. Bovenizer wanted to be helpful, so when someone passed him the cell number Sherlock was leaving around, Bovenizer texted him, and soon they spoke.

Bovenizer didn't think he could be that helpful, as he hadn't witnessed anything himself. But he thought Sherlock should know something. He had a second cousin named Brian Gilmartin, who was the son of a man named Chuck Gilmartin, who was Bovenizer's uncle and Hughes's uncle. Chuck Gilmartin was also the man who had identified Hughes' body at the morgue. David Gilmartin, the good friend of John Hughes and Larry Raddatz, was another of Chuck's nephews.

As the murder investigation was floundering, Chuck Gilmartin, who was a lawyer himself, had done some investigating on his own. He had done what he could for the family at the time, including trying to get a civil case off the ground and helping to talk to Mestrovic before she went to the grand jury.

There was a file of what had been quietly collected, Bovenizer told Sherlock. Another lawyer named Jimmy Gorman had given Brian Gilmartin a copy of it just months before Gorman died, and Gilmartin still had it. Did Sherlock maybe want to look at it?

"Wait, what?" Sherlock said, not believing his good fortune.

When he got Brian Gilmartin on the phone, he learned it was true. Gorman had passed him a copy of the file in December 2015, maybe knowing that his health was failing and wanting it preserved in the event anyone ever needed it. Gilmartin had taken it to his workplace, an asset management company on Clark Street, and had never even looked at it. The collection of old paperwork was still sitting there.

Gorman had never really said why he wanted Gilmartin to be

the one to have the papers. Maybe because he knew Gilmartin's father also had investigated the Hughes case. He had only made one request: "Just keep it."

Soon it was in Sherlock's hands. It was stuffed with reports that had never been included in the CPD master file for the Hughes case, and how Jimmy Gorman or Chuck Gilmartin had gotten them mattered little. Sherlock inventoried the file, restoring much of the paperwork to the official record, and it felt good. Whoever had whitewashed it before was no longer going to have that victory. Inventory #14352738 was back where it belonged.

"The Gorman file," as Sherlock came to call it, was enough paper to fill a large legal accordion folder, and included a mishmash of actual police reports, supporting documents, detective notes, Gorman's handwritten updates, and newspaper clippings. Sherlock's attention was immediately drawn to the police documents, mostly because they were in the file at all. Much of what he saw had either never made it to the official Hughes file or apparently been purged later.

One sheet slipped among the first dozen or so pages carried a date of May 17, 1976, just two days after Hughes was killed. RELEASE PRISONER was the title of the form, right at the top. The document stated that a seventeen-year-old by the name of Nick Costello had been arrested by officer John Furmanek, confirming part of what Furmanek had told the FBI in 2005.

"Above arrested for investigation into the fatal shooting of John Hughes which occurred at Root & Lowe on 15 May 1976," it continued, in typed letters. "Insufficient evidence to place any charges at this time."

And beneath that, another interesting note. The form had space for someone to type witness names beneath the heading "Persons who viewed subject." And someone in fact had typed a name there: "Mary F. Mestrovic."

So someone in the Ninth District had made a record of Mestrovic positively identifying Costello as being in the car the shot was fired from.

The form requested that the subject, Costello, be released immediately. It was signed by Lieutenant Joseph Curtin, one of the ranking leaders, along with Townsend and Haberkorn, who—per Furmanek's version of events—had gone off to meet by themselves after Mestrovic identified Costello. According to the sheet, Costello had been arrested at 4:17 PM and was out by 9:15 PM.

Sherlock kept flipping through the file. On June 1 officers picked up two teenage sisters with the last name of Padilla and wrote a memo for Lieutenant Curtin. The older girl was eighteen, and the party on Throop had been for her birthday. Officers apparently asked them to name everyone they could think of who would have been invited or who showed up anyway, information that would have provided a good starting place for detectives.

The sisters named the boys who appeared at the party, listing them by the park they hung out at. "From McGuane Park:" the report stated, followed by a list of twelve names. The third name listed was Rocky LaMantia, and Costello was fifth.

On a list of girls' names was Mary Mestrovic, as well as LaMantia's girlfriend Martha DiCaro. There was no mention as far as the sisters knew of anyone having a gun at the party. And the interviewer made another note in the memo. "Mary wasn't drunk," the writer had typed after talking to the girls.

Sherlock kept turning pages over. There were handwritten notes that appeared to be the results of other interviews with teens who had been moving around after the party the night of the shooting. The notes didn't specify whether they were written by Gorman or other detectives at the time. There were scrawled accounts of memories of hurled insults and who went where in which cars after the Throop party. A white LeSabre. A brown Cutlass. A brown Duster.

Sherlock's eyes flitted across the staccato lines of supplemental reports filed by officers forty years earlier, the kind that had clearly been banged out on real typewriters. One was from the end of June 1976. So some six weeks after the shooting, there were detectives who still were trying to take the Hughes case apart. A few of the names had changed. One report noted that a police investigator "T. Strong" had gotten an anonymous tip about where the gun used in the Hughes case could be found, but it had gone nowhere.

The same report also noted that police had started having some teens sit for lie detector tests, with most not being useful. And then, at the end of the same report, was another note, not about a polygraph but about a brief interview. The subject was a teen who was the girlfriend of a youth named Paul Ferraro, another name Sherlock had seen here and there in the file. Apparently the note was made as a possible alibi.

"She related in summary that Paul had been with her all night with the exception of approximately fifteen minutes where he left her sister's house to get a sandwich at approximately 2330 hours," the report read.

Sherlock stopped. So a teen who had drawn at least some interest by police had been unaccounted for not long before the shooting? And the story was that he had left where he was at 11:30 PM—to get a sandwich?

He kept reading. "She further related that he then remained with her until approximately 0200 hours when they left together for Indiana," the note ended. So this same teen had then left the state, just forty minutes after Hughes was pronounced dead?

Sherlock was having trouble believing what he was seeing. Where was all the paperwork on this lead? Could it still be explored?

Sherlock knew he was going to try. He set out to find members of the girlfriend's family, who he hoped were still living in Bridgeport. His desire to find them only intensified when he learned from the paperwork what car Ferraro often drove.

A green Chevrolet.

There was one teen who was definitely not sitting with any police officer for a lie detector test.

There in the Gorman file was a letter from a lawyer named Anthony J. Onesto, on letterhead from his Loop office on Randolph Street. He was already a lawyer of some note and would go on to represent organized crime associates and corrupt politicians, among others. The letter was addressed to Lieutenant Curtin and was regarding one Rocco LaMantia.

LaMantia had already taken a polygraph exam, Onesto wanted the police to know, and that was going to be that. He was only writing because of the "fine reputation" of Curtin's officers.

"I trust that you and your men will continue to enjoy the fine reputation you now have with the defense bar in this area and honor my rigid demand that you no longer question my client about the Hughes killing—or any other matter," Onesto wrote. "Any attempt to interview him further, particularly by picking him up and bringing him in for questioning, will be regarded as a violation of his rights, both as enumerated in the United States and the Illinois Constitutions. I am aware that Mr. LaMantia has already been interviewed at length by members of the Chicago Police Department."

Sherlock was left scratching his head yet again. If that was true, where were those reports?

Onesto had kept writing. "Lest there be any misunderstanding, when I say I do not want Mr. LaMantia questioned, I mean both personally and by any other means. Nor are his parents or other members of his family, who I also represent, to be questioned. I trust that *no contact whatsoever* will be made with any of the above parties."

So apparently Onesto's order for the Chicago Police Department had included Rocco's father Joseph "Shorty" LaMantia, the reputed mobster. Maybe detectives had gotten the message.

Onesto was nice enough to include the polygraph results for police. And that sheet also had made it to the Gorman file. The test had been performed by something called John Hancock Investigations, a subsidiary of the John Hancock Detective Agency, the letter said. Its logo was the familiar scripted name of the famous president of the Second Continental Congress who made sure King George could read his oversized signature on the Declaration of Independence, and who clearly was not running a detective agency in the 7500 block of North Harlem Avenue.

In the letter were the results of the LaMantia lie detector session. LaMantia had been asked seven questions, the letter said, and the "zone of compairison [*sic*]" method had been used. The questions were then listed, though they carried no question marks:

1. Is your true name Rocco LaMantia (yes)
2. Were you present at the time John Hughes was shot (no)
3. Do you suspect someone of shooting John Hughes (no)
4. Do you know who shot John Hughes (no)
5. Do you know whose car was used in the shooting of John Hughes (no)
6. Did you shoot John Hughes (no)
7. Are you withholding any information from the police regarding the shooting of John Hughes (no, I'm not)

"There was no psychological stress indicative of attempted deception on Mr. LaMantia's examination, other than in question

#7," the John Hancock examiner wrote. "It is possible that he may be in possession of information regarding this shooting. However, let me stress to you that this may be as a result of 'outside issues' involving this particular shooting or merely as a result of his feelings toward the police in general."

Sherlock stared at the paper. So not only had LaMantia been allowed to submit his own polygraph results, they had *included* the part where he apparently didn't answer question seven completely truthfully? And that had triggered no alarms for anyone looking at the case?

Sherlock made sure he wasn't overlooking some pile of reports on leads related to LaMantia and any alleged alibi he had for the night of the shooting. He counted the pieces of paper he had that showed all the effort that went into figuring out the full timeline of where the teenage son of a Chicago Outfit figure had been the night of the shooting: none.

LaMantia had been at the party where the night's events apparently started. And he had quickly lawyered up and refused to cooperate.

6

THE EYEWITNESS

Mary Mestrovic Murrihy was hesitating.

She sat at a dining room table in the home of Ellen Hughes Morrissey, John Hughes's sister. It was a place where maybe she could find enough comfort to do this again. The pathway through her dark memory of John's shooting and its aftermath was laid out before her one more time. People kept making her walk it.

Mary had the appearance of an older lady from her neighborhood who might be better suited to a bridge club than acting as a murder witness. She had clearly dealt with enough nonsense in her day and wasn't eager for more. This time there was a tape recorder, which she did not care for, but she agreed to speak anyway.

She was angry, as much as someone like Mary might express it in her slightly reserved way. And there was a sense of bitterness that she had lost a friend this way and that her life had been so marked by it.

Mary had no interest in taking the focus away from John, she said nervously. She was protective of him, even more than forty years later. They talked about how unusual it was that John would find himself in harm's way, which brought a reaction from Mary. Other teens were closer to the car, she said. John wasn't carrying a bat. "There were a lot of people at the park, and it wasn't anything specific to John," she said, seemingly protecting him again.

Ellen sat at the end of the table with her husband. She was in seventh grade when she lost her brother, who was the seventh of eleven kids in the Hughes house in the 500 block of West Forty-Fourth Street in Canaryville. As they spoke, the women were just blocks away from that family home.

Ellen's memories brought laughter and a momentary release for Mary. The family had shared a single bathroom, and their grandmother had lived downstairs. Family life was as crazy as anyone would imagine in those circumstances, Ellen said, but their parents kept order. "I thought that's how every house was," Ellen said. She recalled her red-haired, six-foot brother as a sort of prototypical Irish American kid from Chicago. Sports were a love, but he had brains too. College surely would have been his route. There had been some dating, though that wasn't such a major part of his life. For Mary's part, they were just friends.

Mary was the first to bring up the park. They were there all the time. "It's what we did," she said. "Played volleyball, softball, whatever was happening there."

The night John died, she had been with him at the party on Throop first. She remembered some of the boys having words over a girl, and they decided to leave. Heading to the park was just the natural next thing to do, and lots of other kids were milling around there.

The look of the park had of course changed in all the years after the shooting. And because she had stayed in the neighborhood, the park had stayed in Mary's life. She had been by it "a thousand, million times." On the north end was a field house, with a large slab of concrete. That was where most of the kids hung out. They laughed and joked, and the boys would play basketball.

A couple of cans of beer? "If you insist," Mary said coyly. How about music? "That was a bad era for music, wasn't it?" she said. The answer was classic rock. Stuff like the Doobie Brothers.

On the night in question, kids came and went, Mary remembered, but she wasn't really paying attention. Teens had arrived from the broken-up party in waves, in whatever cars they could find room in. The guys and the girls were clumped separately.

She sketched out her memory on a notebook that was handed to her. The ball fields, the field house. She drew Root and she drew Lowe, the streets that came together at the park's northeast corner. "There were cars parked here. A bunch of people were just sitting on the cars," Mary said, continuing to fill in the scene with a pen. She had stopped waiting for questions. "Some people were kind of in the park. I'm like around here, with some girls by a car," she continued, circling a rectangle she had drawn near the corner. John was a few cars away.

Another car appeared, moving slowly. Mary didn't remember who saw it first. The car reached the corner, near a crowd of people, many of them her friends. "People rushed to the street, and the next thing you know there was a shot," she said, getting ahead of herself. She had been speaking for only fifteen minutes and seemed to want to get to and beyond the shooting as quickly as she could. She had recounted it with little emotion. Her voice had stayed almost monotone.

Could she back up for a moment? It was a green car, she agreed. She "wasn't good at cars," but there was no question about the color. And the streetlight provided enough light for her to see someone sitting in it when it moved closest to her, before it reached the corner of Root and Lowe and her crowd of friends. "He was in the front seat of the passenger side, and the next thing you know, he ducked down, a gun came out of the car and fired a shot," Mary said matter-of-factly.

"He" was Nick Costello. She knew his nickname, "Horse," and had called out to him when the car got close. Her family had known his family since she was in early grammar school, Mary said. She was one hundred percent certain. It was just a fact that she stated as if there were nothing to debate. She hadn't had to stare into the car and struggle to find a name of someone she thought she might have recognized. She knew him, and that was that. Instant recognition. Mary stated it as if she had said the ocean is blue, and since everyone knows the ocean is blue, why carry on about the blue ocean?

Then Mary came to a full stop. She was still sitting at the table, sometimes looking toward Ellen, and sometimes looking at her hands. It had gone from light outside the house to dark, making the overhead lights seem suddenly brighter. There were other parts of the story to move to, just after the gunshot. But Mary would wait for a question about it.

What did she remember, then, about John being hurt? "Oh," she said, as her voice cracked slightly. A single word into her answer, and pain had crept in. The steadiness was gone, and her voice shook. "Just that he was down on the ground." She took a long pause. "It's terrible. People running different directions. There was no . . . 911. I know there were houses on Lowe. I remember someone running to a house there. And then I don't know," she said.

Minutes passed, she remembered. The police were not there. Exactly when she left Mary couldn't say, but she eventually went home. She was stunned and had no idea that John died that night; she just knew he was going to the hospital.

Again, she said, John was not an aggressive person. It would have been way out of character for him to initiate any trouble and charge the car, an act which she did not see herself. She wasn't close enough to the actual shooting to be able to say if the shooter could have been targeting anyone who wasn't John. There was no hint that she was making her witness account out to be any more thorough than it really was.

"I mean really, technically, they shot into the crowd," Mary said of her view. "I don't know if they had an intended victim."

Ellen sat quietly at the table as Mary recounted what she had seen. As a seventh grader, she had been asleep when her brother was killed. Her memory was her sister, Theresa, then twenty, coming into her room and waking her up to tell her that her brother had died. He had been shot in the park. She remembers little after that, except that she was shaking. She had been awakened from a cold sleep. "Totally not understanding," she said, almost in a whisper. "And shaking."

The days that came next were obviously clouded by pain, and Ellen was only able to wrap her mind around it like someone then in junior high could. She still had a paper route, for example. A neighbor had still managed to yell at her because her Sunday paper had been late that weekend and was so mad she told Ellen she had canceled her subscription. So someone drove her for the rest of the route.

Maybe it was a thing that made some sense when nothing else did. "I had to deliver these papers," she said. There was still a sense of fortitude in her voice. The fact that the paper route still mattered decades later said much about her.

Still, things had changed immediately. "We were grounded, basically forever," she said. She was laughing, but it had the ring of truth. The Hughes family had talked about moving to the suburbs. For the first time, Ellen's older siblings were scared. She was scared, too. Before then, she had been a '70s kid—parents just announced that everyone needed to be home for dinner or at least by dark. The carefree days of that childhood evaporated as the deep loss set in.

The entry of a gun into the usual neighborhood dispute between their older brothers and friends and the Italian kids was also a marked escalation. Before then, the fighting had been of a simpler type—fists in the alley to settle schoolyard disputes. No one could believe a life had been taken right in front of many of them.

Within a few days, most of the teens had gone back to De La Salle and the other high schools. There was instantly talk about who possibly had done it. A name got back to the Hugheses: LaMantia.

John Hughes's wake lasted two days, there were so many people. Then came the funeral. John's mother fainted at one point, an image that stayed seared in the memories of many who already were beside themselves as they prepared to bury their friend. De La Salle closed the day of the service, as teachers were spared standing in front of empty classrooms. The number of attendees was so large, it was impossible to have a luncheon afterward. It felt like most of the residents of both Canaryville and Bridgeport were there.

In a sure sign that the killing and its aftermath took place in 1976, no one recalled a media presence as John was memorialized and laid to rest. Had such a public murder of a star high school athlete from a political neighborhood taken place in a later era, it could have been major news for days, with the family's grief playing across network news and social media on steady loops. Newspapers would have followed every tiny development in the investigation, asking for updates, demanding press conferences, profiling the victim and his family. Teens heading to and from the funeral would have walked around satellite trucks as TV reporters tried to stop them to ask how they were feeling. As it was, Mary could barely recall a single mention in any newspaper, and Chicago still had three major ones—not only the *Tribune* and *Sun-Times* but also the *Chicago Daily News*, which wouldn't shutter for another two years.

Still, the murder seemed to attract a significant amount of police attention, at least at first. Mary remembered being taken by police out of class at Maria High School to the Ninth District. One of the officers was the "T. Strong" who had continually appeared in Sherlock's Gorman file: Terry Strong.

"They came there and took me out of school, without my parents," Mary said.

How did police even know she was a potential witness at that point? "I have no idea." But it was her first recollection of having to deal with the police. Someone in the park could have told officers to find Mary. Her school must have called her mother, Mary acknowledged, because she caught up to Mary at the district station at Thirty-Fifth and Lowe. They were there for a long time, she said, though the years have warped her sense of time.

She was also moved once to the police station at Thirty-Ninth Street and California Avenue, she said. "Seems to me we were in some kind of locker room. I just have a recollection of like, benches, and policemen going back and forth," she said.

Eventually detectives showed Mary a lineup, giving her a minute to see whether she recognized anyone that she had seen the night Hughes was shot. She didn't need it. "It was like I was looking at you," Mary said, motioning toward Ellen down at the end of the table. "They were asking me who I saw. I said, 'I saw Nick Costello. He's there. Right there in the lineup.'"

As far as identifications go, it was as solid as they get. Mary automatically knew who she saw, and her memory had never changed. She wasn't a reluctant witness. Police didn't have to overpromise anything to her or threaten her to pick someone out, as they might if they were trying to flip a codefendant against a friend. But at the same time, her demeanor decades later made it clear she certainly wasn't eagerly pointing a finger at someone she randomly picked to get her own brand of justice. She had lost a friend, sure, but another person she knew had been in the car the shot was fired from. That was all she wanted to tell police, after her mother convinced her. She wasn't accusing him of firing the gun. In all she saw two lineups, she said, the one with Costello in it, and another with no one she knew.

Costello, she saw at one point, was taken from the lineup to an air-conditioned room, where he didn't seem that stressed. She, on the other hand, was taken back to the wooden benches by the lockers. Some officers had been nice to her, she said, but some certainly weren't. Some began to make fun of her within earshot of her and her mother. "There's people laughing all around," Mary remembered, her voice trembling again. "It's like a joke."

One officer she knew was Dave Cuomo. Her mother was an employee of his at the Coral Key, and Cuomo was making sure Mary and her mother didn't forget it as they were being made fun of. "He made some joke like who my mother worked for," Mary said. Cuomo had already talked to her father, after the basement meeting Furmanek told the FBI about. Mary knew Cuomo was making an empty threat, because her father had told Cuomo that Mary would never be kept from helping police and telling them exactly what she saw.

"He made some off-the-cuff joke," Mary said of Cuomo, remembering he teased that she would get in trouble for tattling or something. "Like, 'Oh, if her father finds out—you better hurry up what you're doing—because if her father comes up here, I'm just warning ya. . . .' Something like that." The memory clearly upset Mary, who hung her head for a moment as she fought more tears. "It's not really about my father coming up here," almost as if she were sticking up for herself, still in the police station more than forty years earlier.

She could have used a police ally or a lawyer then, but there wasn't one. She was supposed to be their witness, helping them solve a murder case. The officers who said the worst things didn't say them to her face, but she remained convinced they had said them loud enough for her to hear on purpose. And years later, she still recalled the things they said. "Some of them were calling me a drunk and a slut," Mary said. "They said, 'She knows nothing. It's for attention.'"

Her mother, Rita, was ill at the time, Mary said, and was a

nervous wreck. But that didn't stop some officers from trying to intimidate the pair. But once her sister also arrived at the station at Thirty-Ninth, most of the mocking seemed to stop. Mary did not remember arguing with anyone or yelling that she hadn't been drunk, mostly because no one accused her directly.

At the station on Thirty-Ninth, the car was discussed, the green Chevrolet. Mary remembered believing it was Paul Ferraro's car, but she couldn't tell officers the make and model. She knew it like you knew a friend's or acquaintance's car just by sight, but without paying a lot of attention. Officers at one point took her out to the parking lot, she said, to see if she could point out the car she thought she saw, or a car that might have been the same kind.

"I don't know, I couldn't," she said. "I didn't find it."

It was all confusing, she said, because she thought she had seen the same car around school. She had even looked for it in the days after her ordeal with the police. It hadn't been hard to find. "I remember my friends and I going to the house where Paulie Ferraro lived and looking in the garage," Mary said. "And the car was in the garage."

Mary recalled that months later, she went to talk to the grand jury. She had a clear memory, despite learning from Sherlock that there was no official record of her ever having been there. She couldn't specifically say whether it had taken place at the main criminal courthouse at Twenty-Sixth Street and California Avenue—and, again, she made no attempt to firm up her story by not admitting when she didn't specifically remember some detail. It was this mixture of being firm on important details, not embellishing memories she clearly didn't have, and having to be coaxed to say anything at all that gave Mary and her account so much weight for Sherlock.

"It was a courthouse," she said. "I remember people were sleeping. It disturbed me even at the time. I was a seventeen-year-old kid, and some of the grand jurors were sleeping."

She had been nervous, of course. She remembered a gallery of people. She remembered seeing a court reporter, tapping away as she talked. There was an assistant state's attorney asking her questions, though she couldn't remember each and every one. And, most important, Mary said, she told the grand jury the name of the person she knew who was there that night.

"Was there anyone you recognized in the car?" Mary said the prosecutor asked her.

"And I said yes," she remembered, answering that it was Costello.

The whole thing was over fairly quickly, Mary said. She remembered being surprised by that. She had been expecting to have to search her mind for more answers. There were a lot of questions she thought she should have been asked, but wasn't. It didn't seem very thorough.

Ellen's "Uncle Chuck," her mother's brother, had sat Mary down at one point just to give her an idea of the kinds of questions she might be asked; after all, Chuck Gilmartin was a lawyer and Mary was a teenager. Mary's mother and Ellen's mother were friends, they remembered, and Mary was friends with one of Ellen's sisters. Everyone thought it might be helpful for Mary to have some idea what to expect from the process, but as it turned out, Gilmartin asked her many more questions than the prosecutor at the courthouse did.

Mary did not recall whether anyone she knew had preceded or followed her when she testified. She didn't remember whether she saw any other teenagers there waiting a turn. John's friend, Larry Raddatz, had his own memory of going to a courthouse, but Mary did not remember seeing him on the day she gave her testimony. She had left the grand jury in pretty short order, she said, and while she might have been thanked for her time, nothing stood out in her mind about her departure. She left, and that was that. She never prepped for a trial that never happened. She was never sworn in and asked to repeat what she saw for twelve jurors who would decide the guilt or innocence of someone accused of shooting and killing John Hughes. Life kept going, and so did Mary.

Ellen couldn't remember at exactly what point the family knew there was a problem with the investigation. They had started by thinking they would sit back and let the police do their job. Their neighborhood had a number of police families, and they had never had a reason to be distrustful. Her father was a carpenter and her mother a housekeeper; they didn't have much experience with investigative matters anyway. Uncle Chuck was, at least at first, their best outside chance at making something happen to find justice.

"By the time they realized the police weren't really doing their job, it was really late in the game," Ellen said. "You trust people to do the right thing. I don't know what transpired that they thought there was a problem."

But later in the year that John died, the family did take a step: they hired a private investigator. He was the one who started poking around and came back to the family within days. "He asked my parents to meet him in the backyard," Ellen said. "He really wanted to talk to them but he wanted to go in the backyard. He told my parents that he was strongly suggested not to take on this case."

Exactly who had "suggested" the private investigator move on to other matters was never revealed to the family, but paranoia set in. "My parents thought there was a bug in the phone and cameras in the streetlights," Ellen said. She remembered the episode with the private investigator as a time when it seemed like everyone was going a little nuts. Her parents suspected that the mob was exerting influence over the case—a possibility that scared them. They had ten more children to think of and care for.

She was laughing at the moment, but it was very serious then. Not only had the Hugheses lost a son and then not gotten justice, now they had to worry about some malevolent force inflicting further pain. Their lives continued but were forever changed.

Mary went back to school. She went back to her job, as a cashier at a small grocery store at Thirty-Fourth and Halsted. But she didn't forget about her friend or what she had told police. There were some in Bridgeport who also didn't forget it. Mary said she was periodically harassed over it, mostly by girls in the friend circle of the teenage boys who may have felt threatened by Mary's account of that night. When she was on the register at the grocery store, Mary said, "they would put a bunch of stuff in a cart, and I would check it out, and they would leave" without the items and without paying, making her do extra work for nothing. Once a group waited for her shift to be over and followed her home in a car. They never did anything to her or directly threatened her, but Mary got the message. Her family called police, who gave her mother a business card with a number on it to call in the event things got more serious, Mary said.

For both Mary and Ellen, the killing changed the dynamic of the neighborhood. Families were less trusting. No longer was it a given on a warm night that there would be large groups of friends milling around at Boyce Field, or any other nearby park, for that matter. Mary finished her senior year at Maria, and then went away to school. She attended a small college in the suburbs for a year and then Illinois State, on her way to becoming a teacher. But even by the time she started college, it was over, Mary remembered. For police and the authorities, anyway.

For Mary, it was never over. "This is not about me, if that's what you're trying to do," Mary said. She was laughing with Ellen. She had walked the path through her memory again and come out the other side in the way she had wanted to. She had remembered what happened to her but had wanted to keep the focus on her friend John Hughes, and on the failure by police to bring his family justice. To Mary, her own feelings and struggles were completely secondary.

But really, how did she feel now? It was with her every day? Mary wasn't budging. *"Mmhmm."*

7

DIGGING IN

S herlock continued poring over the Gorman file, looking for anything he could latch onto to move things forward. He was convinced Mary was being truthful, and had gone to his FBI bosses on the strength of her account.

She had seemed unsure of herself at times, but she had been willing to put herself out there and help authorities yet again, despite what had happened to her and her mother and despite not having any closure decades later. She was an excellent witness, he thought, and that's what he ran up the chain at the Bureau.

He was flipping through Gorman's old records when he came to a supplementary report. "Homicide/Murder," it read. "John R. Hughes."

It was dated May 25, 1976. Gorman or someone apparently had considered it important, since when it was copied, someone had left a Post-it note on the first page. On the copy, it appeared as a white square with cursive writing in it, with an arrow pointing to the top of the page: "Nick Costello said he, Ferraro and LaMantia were together per wife statements," the note read. *Wife statements?* Apparently that was a reference to Costello's ex-wife, who had appeared before a grand jury in 2000.

He kept reading. The document appeared to have been filed by Terry Strong, the case investigator. The date was ten days after Hughes had been killed, and it amounted to a summary of everything that had been done by that point to attempt to solve the case. "On 17 May 1976 the investigators were instructed to go into the 009th District on this investigation," it began. "Mary Mestrovic . . . in the company of her mother Mrs. Rita Mestrovic . . . were brought into the 009th District by members of the . . ."

The text on the report stopped for a page jump, and the next page appeared to be missing, but what followed was a typed account of what Mary had first told police. Sherlock hadn't had it the first time he spoke to Mary himself. The summary said Strong had done the questioning, and a partner named John Boyle had typed it. It was noted the time was 1530, or 3:30 PM, on May 17, a Monday, which would track with Mary having been taken from school.

What school she attended and what year she was in were the first thing asked. "Maria High School. Junior," she had answered.

At 1:15 AM two nights earlier, where was she and what unusual thing had taken place? "I don't know the time, I was at Boyce Park at Root and Lowe streets. I was standing on Lowe across from the park gate, the group that I was with was talking about a group from McGuane Park coming down," Mary had said, according to the document. "Then a car came and slowed up and waited for the cars in front of it to leave, then it started up and stopped in the intersection of Lowe and Root," she continued.

"People from Boyce Park started going towards the car. Then I heard a shot and someone said they got Johnny. I went up by where he got shot and some kids threw four or five bats at the car. Everyone said that we had to keep him warm so we put our coats on Johnny and someone said to call the police. After the police came me, George Shinnick, Fred Ramos and someone else I'm not sure went to Shinnick's Tavern and told [John's sister] Kathy Hughes what had happened and then I went home."

Strong asked, when the car pulled up and a shot was fired, how close had she been? "When it first pulled up I would estimate I was about 30 or 40 feet from the car and then when the shot was fired maybe 20 feet."

And did she get a look at anyone inside the car? "At the time I was positive that one of the persons in the car was Nick Costello," Mary said.

What did the car look like and how many people were in it? "It was light green, four doors. I don't know makes of cars but it wasn't too big or too small. There were people in the front and the back, four or five people."

The summary was typewritten on plain paper, with occasional underlining, apparently made by Gorman. Costello's name was, of course, underlined. Sherlock kept reading. "The person that you say you were sure was Nick Costello at the time of the shooting, what part of the car was he sitting in?" Strong had asked.

"Front seat passenger side," Mary answered.

Did she see who actually fired the shot at Hughes? "I seen Costello before the shot was fired and when the shot was fired I wasn't really looking," Mary said.

How long had she known Costello? "Since I was in grammar school four or five years" was the answer.

Had she seen the person she knew as Costello in the station that day? Yes. And was he the same person she had seen in the car the shot had been fired from that killed John Hughes? Yes again.

Mary had told the officers there was nothing she wished to add to her statement, and when asked, told them that she would sign it. "Because it's true," Mary said.

The summary report continued for a few more pages, giving Sherlock a much-needed glimpse into the work that was done in the first few days of the investigation.

The next sheet included a paragraph on Costello being brought into the Ninth District. He had been spoken to in the presence of his father, who apparently had not felt the need to bring a lawyer.

"After being advised of his Constitutional rights, Costello was interviewed by Commander Haberkorn," the report read. "Costello at that time denied participating or having any knowledge in the murder of John Hughes."

He had been confronted with what Mary had said, the report noted, including that he had been in the car the shot was fired from. "Costello again denied any knowledge of this incident and refused at that time to make any further statements in this matter," it continued.

Inside that paragraph, a name was circled: Haberkorn, the commander who had taken a role in the case. Someone had again applied a Post-it note to it, which again appeared as a white box with cursive writing inside. "Haberkorn took over this investigation and pushed dets aside," it read.

"Dets" was clearly short for detectives, and Sherlock agreed with the scrawled note. It would have been highly unusual for someone of Haberkorn's rank to descend into an investigation and insert himself by interviewing a suspect who represented the key lead for the men working the case. The detectives knew best what they had gathered so far, and if Costello or another suspect had agreed to speak to the police, it would be the detectives who would be best positioned to notice inconsistencies or other nuances in the answers.

Whoever typed this part of the report had made sure to include the fact that Haberkorn did the interview with Costello. To Sherlock, it certainly read like Haberkorn had sat down with Costello and his father, collected a "no comment," and handed it to Strong and Boyle. Since there was no mention in the paragraph of a lawyer, there might have been an opening to press Costello and convince him that his best option for saving himself from facing possible charges himself could be to tell what he knew, if anything, about the shooting, especially since the best witness against him was not naming him as the shooter.

Both Mary Mestrovic and Nick Costello were then taken to Area Three the same day, the report stated. That accounted for Mary recalling that she was moved once after starting to talk to police. The key state's attorney supervisor had responded there, read Costello his rights, and collected another refusal to talk. The supervisor had said he didn't believe there was enough evidence to proceed, the report said, so Costello was photographed, fingerprinted, and released from the Ninth District.

The summary next said both Larry Raddatz and his friend John Russell were interviewed the same day. They had described the car as a green Chevrolet two-door. "They further related that they could not identify the passenger in the auto. Raddatz stated that he did not have a clear view of the passenger, but stated that the subject had light brown hair, parted in the middle approximately collar length," the report read. It was no identification, though Sherlock noted it was in the ballpark for Costello.

The next paragraph recounted how Costello had come to be at the Ninth District the night of the shooting. A teen had told detectives he had been at both the party on Throop and the fight in traffic on Halsted. There was no time frame mentioned in the paragraph, but he had told investigators that he had picked up Costello and another teen after seeing them standing at the corner of Thirtieth and Emerald, near McGuane Park. They had proceeded south toward Boyce Field, where they saw a crowd and police on the scene. (There was nothing in the paragraph on whether the group was asked why they chose to go by that park in the early morning hours.) They had been stopped and taken to the Ninth District for questioning.

The next paragraph indicated that four of Hughes's friends who were in the park had been interviewed, a group that included David Gilmartin. None of them could provide a suspect identification, but they agreed on the description of the car.

It was a car much like the one driven by Paul Ferraro, whose name made another appearance in the report next, restating some of what Sherlock had found suspicious. "Paul Ferraro was again interviewed at Area Three headquarters. Ferraro related that he was at his [girlfriend's] cousin's home babysitting during most of the evening and that he only left for approximately 15 minutes at about 2330 hours to get a sandwich. Ferraro stated that he remained at the location until after 0130 hours on the 15th of May and he had no knowledge of this incident," the report read.

"It should be noted that Ferraro had a vehicle similar to that described by the witnesses. [The girlfriend] was also interviewed in the presence of her mother and related the same account as did Ferraro. Both Ferraro and [his girlfriend] agreed to submit to a polygraph examination if necessary."

Someone, apparently Gorman, had paid special attention to the paragraph, perhaps noticing what Sherlock did years later. He had circled the part of it that read "at the location until after 0130 hours." This time was not long after Hughes was shot.

To Sherlock, the implications were clear. The babysitting alibi covered the key parts of the timeline in the murder, to be sure, and it could very well be true. But there was a little more in play. Where had the car been during that time? That would take more digging.

The report closed with several more paragraphs from a number of witnesses, most of whom couldn't add much to the narrative for police. One said he believed the driver had done the shooting with a chrome gun and that he had "curly type hair." Others questioned included some teens who simply had been in cars stopped near

Boyce Field that night. But those interviews did include the youth who was picked up along with Costello at Thirtieth and Emerald after the shooting.

That young man "related that he had been at the party and later at the fight at 31st and Halsted streets," the report read. He "further related that he had been at the park [McGuane] and heard Costello state that he [Costello] would shoot somebody at Boyce park."

Whoa, Sherlock thought. That statement was given May 19, 1976, two days after Costello and Mary Mestrovic had been at Area Three and Costello had been let go. So police had one witness, apparently a friend, telling them he had overheard Costello saying he would shoot someone at Boyce and another witness putting Costello in the car. Costello hadn't provided any alibi.

So why had the case gone cold?

Jimmy Gorman and Chuck Gilmartin also knew the importance of the car. That was obvious from the Gorman file. Their papers were filled with notes about it, including at least two attempts to find and catalog every Chevrolet registered to anyone in the area. It was every car that could even come close to matching the description. Some sheets had dozens of handwritten lines, organized by VIN.

"Location between 200 West to 1800 West, 2200 South to 5100 South," one note read. "71–74 Chev."

One or both men had drawn borders around a good piece of the city grid, including Bridgeport and Canaryville, and had run the vehicles. The list included the name and address of the person each Chevrolet was registered to. But there was no line for the car's color, meaning finding the green ones probably required quick runs within the search perimeter to try to lay eyes on any that might be registered to someone connected to the case. Gorman and

Gilmartin had run their search in reverse as well, looking for cars registered to people with last names they knew were tied to the case, including LaMantia, Costello, the teen who had been picked up with Costello, and the young man who had been struck with the bat during the fight.

Next in the file came more reports on whom police had brought in for polygraph exams. One was both a friend of Rocky LaMantia's and a relative of his girlfriend. This young man "was given four polygraph tests. There were significant emotional disturbances indicative of deception in this subject's polygraph records when he was questioned regarding his knowledge of this particular crime. There were however, no significant emotional disturbances indicative of deception on the questions pertaining to his actual participation in this crime."

Another was the teen whose beating with a toy bat had escalated things that night. He had been given six tests, one report stated. "This subject's polygraph records are erratic to the extent that the examiners are precluded from eliminating him as a suspect in regard to the crime under investigation. However, due to the fact that the subject was suffering from a cold and appeared somewhat fatigued at the time of testing, it is suggested that he be re-examined at a later date if the investigators deem it advisable."

And apparently investigators had kept John Russell on their radar, despite him being the victim's friend. "This subject's polygraph records were unemotional to the extent that a definite decision regarding his status in this investigation cannot be made at this time." Russell's continued inclusion in the investigation would anger his friends even many years later.

Then came information on LaMantia's supposed polygraph. It was in the form of a police report noting the registered letter that had been received from his lawyer, Anthony Onesto, informing the police department that LaMantia had passed one and to leave him alone.

The report noted Onesto had told police he knew LaMantia had been questioned, which raised Sherlock's curiosity as he looked for paperwork. "Also noted in the letter was the fact that this unit has been advised that Rocco LaMantia will not cooperate with the police without first advising his attorney Mr. Onesto," the report read. "It should be noted that as of this writing no person [here] has in fact spoken to Mr. LaMantia."

So at least that was one explanation for why there wasn't a pile of interview notes with a teen who had become a prime suspect in the case, but it still left open major questions about how thorough the police had been. What was emerging to Sherlock was that detectives on the ground like Strong and Boyle appeared to be doing their due diligence, while higher-ups were putting a brick on their efforts. Much more pressure should have been applied to each youth in the circle around this shooting. Those who said anything should have been locked into grand jury statements. Someone would have cracked, he thought; these were teenagers. At times, the police in the Hughes case seemed to be acting like the case was more mysterious than it was, as if they were looking for the Zodiac Killer.

One thread Sherlock knew he had to pick at was the case's links to organized crime. With the possible shooter being the son of an Outfit figure, it was a natural move for him to begin looking into the LaMantia family, including who they knew that could have helped to shield Rocky LaMantia from any prosecution.

His predecessor had done the same. As Sherlock was leafing through Gorman's file, he found newspaper clippings on Michael "Big Mike" Sarno, also known as "the Large Guy," a mobster who, according to the federal government, led a Cicero street crew that allegedly made thousands of dollars a week collecting money from illegal video gambling machines at local bars. The FBI knew he was the main reason an explosion ripped through the front of a competing business called C&S Coin Operated Amusements in neighboring Berwyn in 2003. Turns out nothing gets the feds' attention like setting off a crude pipe bomb in the middle of a busy suburb, and Sarno and his crew were taken down and linked to Outfit-connected operations including heists at jewelry stores. Sarno already had a racketeering conviction in his past, having been convicted along with noted Outfit member Ernest "Rocco" Infelise years earlier.

The case against Sarno included evidence gathered from the bugging of a Cicero pawn shop linked to a member of the Outlaws Motorcycle Club that served as a base for the crew, which was blamed for robberies at jewelry stores across the western suburbs that netted them hundreds of thousands of dollars. The ring went as far as using corrupt police officers to tap into databases and give them information on law enforcement efforts to stop them. One Berwyn officer notably spray-painted a burglary target's garage himself so he could stop by while on duty to case the house. Sarno eventually was convicted and sentenced to twenty-five years in prison.

Swept up in this federal grab bag of mob-related foolishness was one Casey Szaflarski. Szaflarski was in his fifties in 2009 as the case was coming down. The feds accused him of being the guy who went around to the bars, taverns, and clubs where the ring had machines, collecting the cash and making out fake receipts so the proceeds could be skimmed. A jury ultimately found him guilty of aiding and abetting a gambling operation, and he was sentenced to more than three years in prison.

But before his conviction, Szaflarski was trying to be released on bond in 2010, and he put up his Bridgeport home to make it happen. One clip Sherlock found detailed how prosecutors were asking questions about Szaflarski's shady finances, and how he had links to a Chicago police officer. That was why the story had made it into the Gorman file.

Szaflarski was the son-in-law of the late Chicago mobster Joseph "Shorty" LaMantia, according to one report Sherlock found, and the officer was LaMantia's niece.

Gorman was noting the link, albeit by marriage, between the LaMantia family and the officer's family name. Paul Ferraro's girlfriend in 1976 shared that last name, and she had provided Ferraro's alibi. Maybe she could account for the green Chevrolet that some suspected had been used in the John Hughes murder, Sherlock thought. Finding a member of the family to talk about that night was moving up on Sherlock's to-do list.

Mentions of the car continued in the Gorman file. One police progress report included notes on other interviews done with other teens who had been brought in for questioning after being stopped in cars around Boyce Field after the shooting.

"After advising them of their constitutional rights, we interviewed the youths from McGuane Park. Their accounts of the evening's incidents agreed with the accounts given by witnesses," the report read. "They stated, however, that they knew of no one who had a gun or who intended to shoot anyone."

The teens had named some who were in the fight at Thirty-First and Halsted and some who were at McGuane Park before someone apparently drove from there to Boyce and killed Hughes. "When asked about the wanted auto, they stated that the only person in the McGuane Park area they knew had a car that fit the description of the wanted auto is one Paul Ferraro . . ." the notes continued. "They stated, however, that they believe he left for Indiana late in the evening of 14 May. They said he drives a 1973 Chevrolet 4-door Impala, green with a dark green vinyl top. They could add nothing further."

One of the earliest references to the car in the Gorman file came in the form of a typed memo to Lietenant Curtin from May 21, 1976, less than a week after the shooting. It was a summary of sorts from two officers who were working the case, though not Strong or Boyle. They had been to Boyce Field, apparently to work the rumor mill. They even interviewed two "playground supervisors" who "had nothing new."

But the third paragraph stopped Sherlock. "We received information from a person who would not identify himself that the shooter was driving Ferraro's car and that Ferraro was the passenger," the memo said, apparently referencing an anonymous phone call. "The shooter is supposed to be someone by the name of LaMantia."

The caller thought LaMantia was a graduate of De La Salle, Hughes's high school. The officers had shown up at the school to look through recent yearbooks, and found that Rocky LaMantia was still enrolled, and in Hughes's class. They also learned that LaMantia lived nearby, had a juvenile arrest for battery, and had been stopped for a traffic violation the day after the shooting. He would be investigated further, the report said. "We went to gun registration and ran the name of LaMantia and it lists 6 LaMantias with Smith and Wesson revolvers," it continued. "These people will be checked to see if any of the guns are missing."

Witnesses in the immediate days after Hughes was killed had been unable to identify LaMantia or anyone else as the shooter. And those who had been pointed to as being part of the dispute that night had either refused to cooperate or denied any knowledge about the killing in the park. That included Costello, who had refused to answer any questions after Mary Mestrovic identified him as being in the shooting car. And while later witnesses had placed LaMantia at the Throop party and as part of the fight on Halsted, this memo may have been the first indication of anyone signaling that LaMantia could be the shooter. Clearly, even police officers who had been canvassing the neighborhood and working the case had acted as if LaMantia was a new name to their ears.

The report continued with more tipsters suggesting Paul Ferraro had a car like the green one that kids in Boyce had seen. The officers noted the Ferraro family owned three cars, including a Buick, but suggested none of them was a match. On the next line, however, they wrote, "Information obtained also is that Ferraro just before the shooting bought a Chevrolet like the one wanted and the same colors and would . . . have no license," apparently meaning it wouldn't have been registered yet. Some witnesses in the park had told police it was possible the car they saw did not have a license plate.

The report ended with a note that information out of McGuane Park was that before the shooting and the trouble earlier in the night, boys from Boyce had driven by and taunted their rivals, including by shouting out a car window that Martha DiCaro was a whore.

"Martha's boyfriend, main squeeze is a Rocky," the officers wrote that they had learned. "Maybe Rocco LaMantia."

As Sherlock worked his way through the last of the Gorman file, he came to realize it probably was not going to provide him with "the golden egg" he had hoped would be in there, a piece of paper with someone confessing to the killing or specifically pointing a finger at LaMantia or someone else.

What it was providing, however, was a road map of sorts. He could now see approximately what the officers who worked the case at the time had seen, and he could plan his next moves. He could tell that the detectives who had been closest to the investigation were taking it seriously. They had fairly quickly drawn a tight circle around those who were probably involved in some way, only to have their grip on the case loosened by their bosses, who appeared to have had their own motives for easing certain targets out of the police dragnet.

The efforts of the detectives included steps common in that kind of investigation, such as having a composite sketch made of a possible shooter. To have it made though, they chose to bring in John Russell, one of the Hughes friends who had acknowledged not getting a great look at the passenger in the shooting car. But Russell had also told police that if he ever saw the shooter again, he might be able to identify him. That was good enough. But there was no record of the sketch being released to the media. Instead it appeared in a police newsletter in July 1976, showing a somewhat thin-faced White male with darker hair and defined eyebrows.

Unknown M/W, 20–25, olive complexion, short dark curly hair, clean shaven, armed with long barrel silver revolver, driving a 1970–73 light green 2 door Chevrolet with damage on right rear fender and roof. Wanted for the fatal shooting which occurred at Root St. & Lowe on 15 May 76. Reference R.D. X178274. Auth: Area 3 Homicide/Sex Section, CID.

Oddly, the description given was of a man years older than any teen police had been looking at in connection with the case, and clearly older than any of their leading suspects at the time. It also authoritatively stated the car in question would have dents, ostensibly from being hit by hurled bats, although witness accounts were not consistent on whether the car actually had been struck as it sped away from the shooting.

The detectives appeared to have done a good job chronicling their interviews with anyone who hadn't blocked them by hiring a lawyer, such as LaMantia. Remaining interviews in the Gorman file included write-ups of their talks with the teen struck by the toy bat earlier in the night, and with Paul Ferraro, whose car was emerging as an investigative route Sherlock hoped to follow to find the truth about what had happened. Sherlock was interested in hearing how Ferraro had described his night at the time and how his car had been accounted for—or not. How had he explained his sudden exit to Indiana with the green Chevy, inside of an hour after Hughes had been shot?

The teen who had been beaten with the toy bat was a seventeen-year-old student who went to De La Salle himself, and he had been interviewed in the days after the killing with his parents present, according to one report. He acknowledged much of what police had pieced together by that point, but denied knowing about the shooting or being in the car when it happened.

His evening had started at the party on Throop, he said. He had gone there with several friends, including the teen who would later tell police he had overheard Costello talking about shooting someone at the park. The friends he named included Costello, but notably excluded any mention of LaMantia, who had been placed at the party by a number of other witnesses.

"After leaving the party about midnight they all went to McGuane Park. While they were there a group of youths from Boyce park rode by in an auto and made a remark," the police wrote, summarizing what the teen had said. "He then along with the other youths in his company got into their auto and followed them. They caught up with them at Thirty-First and Halsted where a fight ensued."

As he spoke to police, the teen also removed LaMantia from being at the fight. "During this fight [the teen] stated that he was hit by an unknown youth and knocked out. The police arrived and broke up the fight and he and his friends went back to McGuane Park. While they were there they decided to go to Boyce Park and look for the other youths who had beat him up. At this time the police came and told them to go home," the report said, but apparently they didn't obey. "Then he and all of the aforementioned youths went to 30th and Emerald and there left in three autos to go to . . . Boyce Park to fight the previously mentioned boys."

When he arrived, though, the teen said, police were already in the park, and he noticed that other cars belonging to friends from his group were being stopped. He left in a car with three others, he said, and they went back to their own neighborhood. He rode around until 3 AM, he told the detectives, and then went home. He said he didn't hear Hughes had been shot until noon the next day. "He denies having any knowledge of this incident or who owns the wanted vehicle in this case," the accounted ended.

Ferraro appeared to have been interviewed the following day. He was eighteen, a police report on that questioning said, and was working at the time as a pressman. His father sat in as detectives talked to him and advised him of his rights.

Ferraro told the detectives he had no idea why Hughes had been shot a few nights before.

"Do you own or have access to a 1972 Chevrolet auto, green in color?" they asked.

"Yes."

"Was that auto in your control on the night of 14 May 1976 and the early morning of 15 May 1976?"

"Yes."

"Did anyone else have access or control of that auto on the times mentioned in the previous question?"

"No."

The detectives asked Ferraro to tell them about his activities that night. "At 9 PM I was babysitting with my girlfriend at her cousin's house across the street from where my girlfriend lives," Ferraro said. That was the girlfriend whose family name Gorman had linked to Shorty LaMantia, and she lived on Emerald.

They'd been at her cousin's house babysitting from 9:00 PM until 1:30 AM, Ferraro told them, according to a transcript of the interview included with the report Sherlock read.

Had he left at any time? "Yes I left at 11:30 pm and went to Connie's restaurant at 26th and Normal to get a hamburger." Ferraro said he had only been gone for fifteen minutes. After the babysitting ended, Ferraro said he and his girlfriend had walked back across Emerald to her house, where they had stayed until 2:10 AM that Saturday morning.

"Where did you go then?"

"My girlfriend and I and my girlfriend's mother and aunt left for Warsaw, Indiana," Ferraro told the officers. There was no follow-up question about why they would do that at such an odd time. In Sherlock's mind, the scenario was suspicious, and police at the time should have taken it apart down to the minute. The car alone should have warranted closer scrutiny. Here was a friend of some who might have been involved, and he had a car matching the description of the shooting car that he had said was in the area.

Ferraro told the officers who were interviewing him that he had seen only the people they were babysitting for during the time he was discussing.

"Do you have any knowledge of how or why or who shot John Hughes?" the detectives asked as they wrapped up.

"No," Ferraro said.

It was not a terribly long interview, and no one had accused Ferraro of being involved in the shooting itself. But Sherlock remained very interested in the car. There was a note in the same police report that the family had volunteered to have it looked at, and that no dents from hurled bats were found. Despite the witnesses' inconsistency on this point, police apparently were again looking for a vehicle with rear damage.

But Sherlock noticed one thing almost instantly. Ferraro had said the babysitting job was in a particular block of South Emerald. In the report detailing how Nick Costello came to be scooped up near Boyce Field the night of the shooting, the driver of the car Costello was riding in had told detectives he picked up Costello and another teen after seeing them standing at Thirtieth and Emerald, just blocks from the babysitting job and Ferraro's car. If the vehicle had been borrowed and used in the shooting, there was plenty of time to have left it back where Ferraro was. It was certainly very possible to Sherlock that Costello had accepted a ride back to Boyce to casually see if someone had been injured by the gunshot or just to avoid suspicion.

Sherlock also knew that if the car had been involved in the shooting, it would explain the sudden desire of Ferraro and his girlfriend's family to drive it to Indiana less than an hour after Hughes was pronounced dead at Mercy Hospital. Sherlock wasn't fully aware of what the full family connections might be between the LaMantias and the family of Ferraro's girlfriend. But if there were dots to connect, police hadn't done it, or supervisors had tamped down the effort.

It was time to chase a car, Sherlock thought, but not in any normal police pursuit. The vehicle he wanted to track probably had been in a junkyard for twenty years. He started by looking for Ferraro and the family of his girlfriend. In a computer search he found a woman with the same last name, still in the neighborhood, who was old enough to be the mother of Ferraro's girlfriend. It would have been her house on Emerald the group had left, apparently to go to Indiana in the middle of the night, all those years ago.

The older woman had moved since then. She lived in a small, tidy brick home along a park, just a stone's throw from Midway Airport. Sherlock had no idea what to expect when he walked up a few concrete steps to knock on the door.

8

MARTHA

On May 6, 1979, just shy of three years after John Hughes was shot and killed, a gunshot rang out inside a house in Bridgeport at 2812 South Shields.

It was almost 9 PM when a 911 call went to a police dispatcher, with a young man's frantic voice on the line. "Get an ambulance here right away. I need an ambulance right away," the caller said. "I got . . . someone got shot in the mouth. How do I stop the bleeding? Just come here. I done . . . it was a mistake with a gun. It's a girl, she's young . . . Come here, please."

The dispatcher tried to make sure they knew where he was.

"2812 South Shields. It's a house," the caller said. "Please hurry up . . . please. It's my girlfriend."

The caller was Rocco "Rocky" LaMantia, by then twenty years old. The simple one-story brick walk-up with a bay window was the LaMantia home, where Rocky still lived with his mother and his father, Joseph "Shorty" LaMantia.

Police officers raced to the call of a person shot, arriving within minutes. They were greeted by Shorty, who was standing in the street to meet them. "It was an accident," he told them.

It turned out Shorty had not been home at the time of the shooting. He had been at a communion party at a club called Garibaldi's on Twenty-Sixth Street, where Rocky had called for his father before calling 911.

The officers walked up the stairs and went inside to see for themselves, according to police reports. They found Rocky kneeling over a teenage girl in blue jeans and a yellow blouse. She had been shot in the left side of the face, just at the corner of her lips, and obviously wasn't moving. Two more officers had arrived by then, and they saw Rocky with blood on his right hand, telling the girl over and over, "Don't die. Don't die."

The girl on the kitchen floor was Martha DiCaro, his longtime girlfriend. She was nineteen, and she was already dead.

The officers pulled Rocky up and told him to give her some space. Shorty entered the room and asked to talk to his son outside. The cops allowed him to do that, and overheard Shorty as he ushered his son back to the front door. "Keep your mouth shut," Shorty told Rocky. "Don't say anything."

Minutes later, they went outside and placed Rocky in one of their squad cars. And he did say something. His initial call to 911 about a mistake with a gun was irreconcilable with the statement he now gave. He told police two men had come into the home wearing nylons over their faces, and they had been the ones to shoot Martha. They wore baseball jackets, he said, and one had on a western-style belt.

LaMantia said he had been in the bathroom. When he walked out toward the house's living room, Martha had been just in front of him. As they walked out, they were confronted by the two men, and one of them raised a pistol. A shot struck Martha in the face, knocking her back into him, he told officers, and the men fled.

Police detailed the account in a report. "He then stated he made Martha comfortable and first called his father who was attending a communion party," they wrote. "He then called 411 who told him to dial 911, and he then dialed 911 and notified police."

Some of the officers at the house then spread out into the neighborhood, looking for anyone who might match the description of the two men LaMantia described.

Just then, Rocky's brother appeared, and found him in the squad car. "Rocky, what did you do?" his brother said, as the two young men began to fight. Officers saw Rocky kicking at his brother from inside the car, and their father rush over to break it up.

"I have the lawyer, don't say anything," Shorty told Rocky again, as officers stood nearby. "I know what the lieutenant is trying to do. Don't say anything."

Rocky then began throwing up in the car before he was taken away to Area One police headquarters for questioning.

Officers who had fanned out through the nearby streets found no home invaders with nylons on their faces. A Ms. Kostecka had been sitting on the front steps of her building for much of the prior hour and had a clear view of the front of the LaMantia house. No unusual men had come in or out.

That's because there weren't any. The story had changed again. Back at Area One, LaMantia's lawyer, Anthony Onesto, the same one who had told police handling the Hughes case to leave his client alone, was telling officers there that LaMantia wouldn't be talking to them. DiCaro had come to the LaMantia home to visit Rocky, Onesto told police. During the visit, she found a gun in Shorty's bedroom and had asked her boyfriend how to use it. Rocky supposedly had refused and taken it from her. She had tried to take it back, Onesto said, and when she grabbed for it, it went off by accident.

How Martha had wound up in the kitchen wasn't accounted for. Officers also had been to Mercy Hospital, where Martha had been taken. They viewed her body, and noted a "star effect wound" to her face. It was another way to describe a contact wound. The end of the barrel of the gun had been pressed right to her mouth when the trigger was pulled.

One of the detectives working the case that day was named Kunz, and he had also worked the Hughes case. What he might have thought at the time about what had unfolded with one of the main suspects from the Hughes murder was unknown, as nothing was noted in police reports from that day. There was also nothing noted later, when the bullet was recovered from inside DiCaro's skull. It had entered near her mouth and traveled upward into her brain, but had never exited. It was determined to have been fired from a .32 caliber Smith and Wesson long revolver, the same gun police suspected had been used in the Hughes murder.

Any thought Sherlock had to find records on a forensic analysis of the weapon quickly faded. They did not exist. That's because the weapon was never recovered, despite the LaMantias' story being that Martha died in an accidental shooting while struggling for Shorty's pistol—as opposed to masked intruders killing her and leaving with their own murder weapon. Shorty LaMantia had beaten the police to the house, that much was clear. So whatever happened to the gun that allegedly was from his bedroom would remain a mystery. And without access to the weapon that killed Martha DiCaro, investigators certainly couldn't link it to the Hughes killing, a possibility that definitely would have been on the mind of Kunz and any other officer aware of both shootings.

Investigators quickly began piecing together the troubled five-year relationship between Rocky and Martha. Members of her family were interviewed by two assistant state's attorneys at Area One. Mavis DiCaro, Martha's mother, told them her daughter had been trying to break things off. "Each time she would try, he would become very angry and threaten her, her mother's safety or some other family member's safety," a police report on the conversation noted. "Because of these threats, the victim would go back with Mr. LaMantia."

There had been some physical abuse, Mavis DiCaro said; the police noted that no domestic violence complaints had been filed.

The DiCaro family had occasionally told Shorty about his son's behavior, and he would speak to Rocky.

Martha's mother also told police about an incident just a few weeks earlier. Martha had shown up at her mother's workplace, a currency exchange in suburban Berwyn, because Rocky had said he was coming over and Martha was afraid. She had hurried in and gone around to stand behind the business's bulletproof glass.

"When Mr. LaMantia came in, he was very abusive to both women and threatened them both," the police report stated. Mavis DiCaro had tried to call the LaMantia family but eventually had to call the police. Again, no complaint was filed, and officers had just told LaMantia to move on.

After LaMantia stopped cooperating with police and prosecutors looking into the DiCaro murder, a decision was made to hold him while Martha's brother and girlfriends were interviewed. Two investigators, including Kunz, also returned to the LaMantia home on Shields. There were a couple of things they were looking for: the gun, obviously, and a white sweater Rocky had been wearing when his girlfriend was shot. When they arrived, Shorty was there, and they asked about the sweater.

"There is no sweater," he told them, according to a report they made.

When they asked about the gun, they got a similar reply. Shorty said he wouldn't be answering any more questions until he spoke again to Onesto, the family's attorney. Police officers asked if they could just go inside themselves and look around, and they got the same answer. Shorty called Onesto and came back and told Kunz and his partner they would need a warrant.

Other officers were more successful. Martha's ten-year-old brother Paul, a fourth grader at a Catholic school near the family's home in Cicero, told police Rocky sometimes came to the house and threatened his sister and his mom.

"He stated that Rocky would take his sister into her bedroom when he would come over and he was unable to see if Rocky would do anything to her," one police report said.

Officers also were interested in an account given to them by a Kirk Delise, a nineteen-year-old who was working at the Sportsman's Park horse track in Berwyn. In the on-and-off tumult of the DiCaro-LaMantia relationship, Delise had gone out with Martha during one of the off moments. A few months later, about a year before her death, he had been at her house paying her a visit when Rocky had come by. "Enjoy your meal, it will be your last," Rocky had apparently said to Delise, before taking Martha into her bedroom for fifteen minutes. She had emerged with red marks on her neck, Delise recalled.

The altercation had continued, with Rocky allegedly threatening to hit Delise with a plate before the two stepped outside. According to Delise, Rocky had reached toward the side of his pants and threatened to shoot Delise, who told police he told Rocky to go ahead in front of everyone who was there. By that point, some of Delise's friends whom he had called from the house had arrived. Things deescalated, but Delise told police Rocky would occasionally call to threaten him.

Delise told investigators he had been at the club called Garibaldi's with Martha's brother Charles just a few days before Martha was killed. It was the same neighborhood hangout where Rocky would call his father after the shooting. Delise said he had seen Rocky there, and that Rocky had asked him whether he had seen Martha in Florida earlier in the year. Delise had been there at the same time.

"Delise told him that he had seen her one time at the Limelight while they were in Florida," police wrote in a report on the interview. "LaMantia told him that he was going to get engaged, buy a house, and open a car wash, and that if he ever caught Martha DiCaro fucking around he was going to shoot her and whoever she was with, and that his old man would pay $20,000 to get him off."

Police interviewed Charles DiCaro as well, who told them he and Rocky had a discussion after the confrontation with Delise at the DiCaro house. Rocky and Charles were from the same neighborhood, Rocky argued, so Charles shouldn't let Delise and his friends gang up on him. Charles told officers he had replied that Rocky shouldn't bully Delise, and Rocky had shown him a gun, saying he wasn't worried about it.

Also on the interview list were two of Martha's friends, who described a troubled relationship between her and Rocky. One of them was a girl named Sandra Parrilli, who told police she spoke with Martha several times a week. On Sunday, May 6, Martha was supposed to call after going to see her grandmother and then going to Rocky's house; it was a call Parrilli would never get.

"She stated that on Saturday, May 5, she had spoken with Martha and she had stated that Kirk had said he met LaMantia in Garibaldi's lounge and LaMantia had told Kirk that he if ever caught her cheating he would kill her and the guy she was with," police wrote in a report. "He had also told Kirk that he was going with several other girls, and at this time Perrilli asked Martha why she did not confront LaMantia with this and Martha stated that she was afraid of what he would do. Sandra Parrilli also related that last summer LaMantia had shown her a gun and it had a brown square handle."

Another friend was Patricia Cavalier, who told police she had been present when Rocky hit Martha. She had also once seen Rocky drag Martha by the hair into an alley and rip a chain from her neck. She had spoken to Martha the week before the shooting. "Martha had told her that LaMantia had threatened her with a gun by pulling it out and pointing it at her and stating, 'I will shoot you,'" police noted.

Officers stamped their case CLEARED BY ARREST and CLOSED. LaMantia was charged with first-degree murder and later indicted. Prosecutors would go ahead with a trial on the theory that an enraged Rocky LaMantia had shot his girlfriend in a lovers' quarrel. Rocky, still represented by Onesto, pleaded not guilty.

Martha's family was left to struggle with what had happened. Their dark-haired girl with a bright smile had wound up in the morgue, with a medical examiner removing a spent lead bullet from her head and noting findings about her injuries on a form. They took out a small personal ad in the *Chicago Sun-Times* in July 1979, on what would have been Martha's twentieth birthday.

> Sad and sudden was the call of one so dearly
>   loved by all.
> A bitter grief, a shock so severe, it was to part
>   with one so dear.
> The tears keep flowing every day, it seems the
>   pain won't go away.
> You can't come back, we know it's true, but
>   just remember we'll always love you.
> Mom and Dad

Throughout 1980 and into 1981, Rocky would appear at the Criminal Court Building at Twenty-Sixth and California, along with his lawyer, as his case wound through repeated status dates.

Police were appearing there too. They filled out numerous court attendance reports as they worked with prosecutors to make sure the evidence they had collected was ready to go.

"Had a pretrial conference with Assistant State's Atty. Michael Goggin in regards to the above case," a typical report read. "The [officer] went over his actions both at the scene of this incident and at the Area 1 headquarters. Also the [officer] went over the tape recording of the defendant calling police."

And another: "On today's date . . . had a pretrial conference with some of the witnesses that will appear in this matter." Those witnesses included Paul and Charles DiCaro, the victim's brothers, and her friend Patricia Cavalier, to whom Martha had spoken about Rocky pointing a gun at her. "Also, tendered to the ASAs on this date was a copy of the tape message recorded at the police communication center on the night of the incident. Also, four handwritten love letters from the defendant to the deceased were turned over to the state."

It is not unusual for attorneys to file what is known as a "substitution of judge," or SOJ motion as their cases progress, sometimes alleging a judge has a conflict of interest. Often it's really a bid to find a more sympathetic ear, a practice known as judge-shopping. They will sometimes find success, and a trial will be held before a jurist who didn't have the case initially. But even for criminal court in Chicago, where defense lawyers can judge-shop with the best of them as they try to avoid those with pro-police reputations, it would have taken a scorecard to follow the LaMantia case.

Judge Daniel Ryan had it first, and held a number of pretrial hearings. LaMantia would appear, with paperwork noting he had been released on $60,000 bond. Then in March 1981, with the case moving forward, Onesto, Rocky's lawyer, SOJ'd him. The motion and the case appeared headed toward Judge James Schreier, but Onesto argued both Schreier and another judge in the building, Arthur Cieslik, would be biased against his client.

Once again, the case was moved, this time to a judge Earl Strayhorn. But it would not stay there, either. Just before trial that spring, Strayhorn suddenly recused himself, with court records stating the case had been sent to him "in error." Another judge would handle the trial. That was Thomas J. Maloney. Apparently the fact that Maloney had represented Shorty LaMantia in some matters as a lawyer before he made it to the bench was no obstacle to the case landing in his courtroom.

On April 1, 1981, Rocky LaMantia waived his right to have a jury hear his case. Maloney would hear the evidence in a bench trial, and decide whether Rocky was guilty.

There were several days of testimony as prosecutors presented evidence that Rocky and Martha DiCaro had a turbulent history and that Rocky had threatened her. They had begun dating when the DiCaro family lived in the Bridgeport area, but they eventually moved to Cicero. The couple had grown more estranged, and Martha showed up at Rocky's house on May 6, 1979, to break off their relationship once and for all.

It hadn't gone well. At some point, Martha had ended up with the barrel of a gun pointed in her face—and in fact touching it—near her mouth. The trigger had been pulled, and the bullet ricocheted inside her head, up and through her brain, killing her.

Neighbors testified they had seen Joseph "Shorty" LaMantia before any police, telling the court how they saw Shorty park outside and run into the house. Responding officers testified about the changing story they got. Rocky had initially told the 911 dispatcher Martha was killed in a mistake. Then it was a killing by masked invaders, and finally it was a struggle for a gun.

Evidence had gone missing from the crime scene, including the bloody sweater Rocky was wearing, a purse Martha had carried, and of course the revolver from which the fatal shot was fired.

The defense case was limited, and Rocky LaMantia didn't testify to explain himself. But ultimately it didn't matter. Judge Maloney said he was unconvinced by the state's evidence, and acquitted Rocky on April 10, 1981.

The trial and its outcome was another crushing blow to DiCaro's family. They believed their daughter's killer had walked out of court a free man. *Chicago Tribune* reporter Bonita Brodt covered the case and reported how the DiCaro family embraced as Judge Maloney explained his decision.

"There is little to contradict the defendant's statements. There is nothing to support it and there is a reluctance to accept it," Brodt quoted Maloney as saying, in an apparent reference to the final version of events LaMantia had given investigators through his lawyer. The judge said he found a "void" in the evidence that left him unable to convict LaMantia beyond a reasonable doubt, Brodt wrote.

The possible real motivation behind Maloney's decision would remain secret for years. The DiCaro family had a hard enough time accepting it as it was. Brodt continued to follow the case, and quoted Mavis DiCaro, Martha's mother, for a later story headlined KILLING UNEXPLAINED; FAMILY ASKS, "WHY?"

"Our lives have been destroyed. Ruined. There is nothing for us to look forward to," DiCaro told the reporter. "Something is missing out of our lives that cannot be replaced, and the bad thing is, we have two other kids that now we can't enjoy."

Who knows whether Judge Maloney picked up the paper that day and read the quote from a grieving mother. Maybe he folded the paper at his kitchen table that morning over his corn flakes and felt a twinge of guilt as he looked down at the text. Or maybe he just set the paper down and enjoyed his breakfast. Maybe to him, if something nefarious had happened, it was just business, albeit the worst kind of business for someone in his profession. He had been a judge for just two years and was building a reputation for being tough on criminals. He would remain on the bench for another ten, handing out tough sentences to many who appeared before him, maybe just for appearances.

Rocky LaMantia wouldn't have to worry about that.

9

THE SOUTH SIDE GROUP

S ix years after his son was acquitted of shooting a nineteen-year-old girl in the face in his house, Joseph "Shorty" LaMantia had a new problem, though he didn't know it yet.

It was 1986 and the federal government had taken aim at something that sometimes went by the harmless-sounding name of "the South Side Group."

But it wasn't an association of local businessmen or a singing company. It was the Chicago Outfit street crew under the authority of Angelo "the Hook" LaPietra, a feared mob boss who had picked up the moniker for his use of a meat hook while torturing enemies of his organized crime ring. The group went by other names as well, including the Twenty-Sixth Street crew, or the Chinatown crew, which better described their geographic Outfit territory. It was a swath of the city south of the Eisenhower Expressway, including Bridgeport and the Chinese neighborhood growing along Wentworth Avenue. The crew, one of six controlled by the leaders of the Outfit, held sway over gambling and high-interest juice loans, collected street taxes from businesses, and tapped into the area's generous supply of truck and train yards.

The South Side Group was also the willing knife of the Outfit. When other crews weren't able to pull off a murder they had been tasked with, leaders knew they could count on the Chinatown crew. It wasn't uncommon for its soldiers to carry out killings well outside of its territory for mob leaders.

The FBI and federal prosecutors were out to build a racketeering case, and were targeting Angelo and his brother James LaPietra. Also on the radar were members of Skids Caruso's old crew and Shorty LaMantia, who was known to the feds to be a manager of sorts for the group's lucrative gambling operations. Some of the crew's moneymaking schemes fed off each other. When gamblers on LaMantia's end got behind on horses or sports wagers, they could take out a high-interest juice loan from another LaPietra assistant, Frank Calabrese Sr. In 1986, Calabrese was known mostly as a guy who put money on the street for the group. It was only later, when his brother Nick flipped in the landmark Family Secrets conspiracy case, that Frank Calabrese would become known as a multiple murderer, taking lives usually by surprising his victims and strangling them with a length of rope.

To make their 1986 racketeering case, prosecutors got permission from a judge to intercept calls between the men and other members of their organization. They began making recordings at an Italian American club that LaPietra had cofounded on Twenty-Sixth Street. The location had been the site of Garibaldi's, where LaMantia took the phone call from his son after Martha DiCaro was shot. LaPietra's club was the first of two he was credited with, the second opening several blocks west a few years later.

The club and LaMantia would come up years later during the Family Secrets trial, with Nick Calabrese recounting years of Chicago Outfit activity and killings. He pleaded guilty and described how a suburban enforcer named Sam Annerino was targeted for death after running afoul of Outfit bosses. Their plan had been for someone to bring Annerino to the new club as it was being renovated, to show him the site. Lying in wait would be Nick and Frank Calabrese Sr., along with Ronnie Jarrett and another Outfit hit man. They had gone to the empty building several times during the evening hours and waited. The someone who was supposed to bring Annerino by, according to Nick, was Shorty LaMantia.

LaMantia hadn't been successful in snaring their target, and Nick described a time Shorty went by the location of the new club, still without Annerino but with LaPietra, while the hit squad was still sitting there biding its time. "And when Angelo walked in and [Shorty] seen us standing there, he got scared," Calabrese had told the jury during the trial. "He turned white because he thought that he was going to be killed."

LaMantia would have had good reason to be afraid, as such Outfit double-crosses were common ways to lure unsuspecting victims. It was a regular ruse to bring someone along as part of a hit team when they in fact were the target. As it turned out, LaMantia had no issue, and he was spared. Nick never said whether they had to calm him down. Members of the crew left to go wait at Jarrett's mother-in-law's house, where Frank Sr. took a call that another crew that had been slow to take care of Annerino had actually come through in the end. No one got whacked at the construction site of LaPietra's Italian American club that day.

The feds captured none of that drama for their 1986 case, however, as their taping effort began years after the club first opened. They also tapped phones at a local tavern and a business known as Sea Hoy Seafoods, where bets were taken. But the Italian American club especially remained a hotbed of criminal activity, the feds said, acting as a headquarters of sorts. Mob business would be conducted there, with cash coming and going and LaPietra controlling things, according to the feds.

They were hoping to gather evidence on it all. The gambling, the street tax, the threats and intimidation. To get permission for the operation, investigators had filed an affidavit that included the results of surveillance operations and information from twenty-two people, including fourteen confidential informants, according to a document that outlined the targets' roles in the organization.

Sherlock didn't have all the details on that particular case, but had heard enough of the local folklore to know who Shorty LaMantia and his cohorts were. Finnigan, his old police teammate who had gotten into his own trouble, was from Bridgeport. Finnigan knew all the tales, very many of them true.

In court filings, including one government response to LaMantia's attempts to suppress what the government had collected, federal authorities outlined the history of each man. Angelo LaPietra had an arrest record that dated to 1938, and his background included a conviction for skimming Las Vegas casinos along with Outfit heavyweights Joseph "Doves" Aiuppa and colorful mobster Joey "the Clown" Lombardo, who would die in 2019 after a long stint in the supermax prison in Florence, Colorado, reserved for terrorists and gang leaders.

LaMantia "had an arrest record dating back to 1951," prosecutors wrote in one filing. "Over the years he had been arrested for tampering with an automobile, burglary, robbery, larceny, theft from interstate shipment, cartage theft, shoplifting, and in 1982 for gambling."

Court documents outlined the intelligence the government had built up in their racketeering investigation, even before they started taping. They included summaries from informants who had turned against the Outfit. One informant who had connected undercover FBI agents to Outfit members in the past had told investigators how the organization was structured, with its various crews dividing up the city.

He stated that "his personal association with Angelo LaPietra extended back 'many years' and that he once helped get LaPietra to the hospital for a gunshot wound LaPietra received after they had participated in a 'score,'" the feds wrote in one filing. LaPietra's crew had once forced a juice competitor out of business by beating him and making him come up with $20,000. The competitor eventually wound up very out of business, as he was later found dead. The informant knew Angelo LaPietra was running lots of rackets, and money that was collected for him went to the club.

Some of the most pertinent information on Shorty himself came from Ken Eto, famous to mob-watchers of a certain age in Chicago as "Tokyo Joe." Eto has a hall-of-fame spot on the list of Outfit turncoats, mostly because he survived an attempted hit by two men that included three shots to the head. If he was on the fence before about becoming a government informant, that incident sealed the deal. And the two men who had tried to kill him wound up in a car trunk themselves for messing it up. Eto knew LaMantia as well, and the feds also used information from him as they built their case. Eto had been involved in illegal gambling for decades and knew that LaMantia was in LaPietra's organization, which he often had to deal with. LaMantia would take bets at a local horse track, he told the government.

Guy Bills also pointed a finger at LaMantia. Bills was a juice loan collector for the Outfit who did work for the LaPietra crew. After he was arrested for stealing from a jewelry store in the 1980s, he rolled for the government and testified against mob boss Alberto Tocco. Investigators noted in court filings that he had been asked about the structure of the Twenty-Sixth Street crew and had named LaMantia as a bookmaker, running gambling operations.

"Mr. Bills stated that 20-25 years ago he was personally present when 'Shorty' LaMantia received a street tax payoff from a 'Chinaman named Wok,'" prosecutors wrote.

The Outfit using Chinatown—and specifically the Cermak Road corridor—as a gambling base was nothing new. It had been doing so for years. The Chicago Crime Commission noted one spectacular episode in its "Report on Chicago Crime for 1962," describing how the chief investigators for the Cook County state's attorney and nearly two dozen cops raided a "big floating crap game" in the 200 block of West Cermak, near the intersection at the heart of Chinatown.

"The first floor of the three-story building at this address houses the G. Consentino bail bond firm and a barbershop. Attached to the building is a one-story structure which contains the First Ward Bureau of Sanitation office," the commission reported. "Eighteen persons were arrested by the raiding officers. Of this number, ten persons attempted to escape through a long tunnel extending beneath a parking lot and leading to the basement of the Chinese Woman's Club at 224 West Cermak Road."

The commission said Skids Caruso was among those who were picked up.

"The officers found three poker tables in the basement and four safes containing $3,000," according to the report. "Of particular interest was a false wall in which the officers located a sawed-off shotgun, a stocking mask, dynamite caps and electrical blasting wire. A cache of burglar tools was discovered including lock pullers, an acetylene torch, an electrical drill, sledge hammers, chisels and various crowbars."

Another notable federal case in the area was the one against the On Leong Chinese Merchants Association. The organization was accused of running what amounted to a full casino in Chinatown, and paying off Chicago Outfit members and Chicago cops to do so. Police regularly raided the group's building in the 1980s, finding upper floors blocked with gates that could be opened when gamblers buzzed in to play fan-tan and other games of chance. In April 1988 operators buzzed in an undercover FBI agent named George Ng, who spoke fluent Chinese and played along with everyone else after buying $500 in chips. Ng came back the next evening with another agent and a search warrant, and a federal complaint was filed that same year.

When the case got to trial, a former national president of On Leong testified the organization paid $12,000 a month in street taxes to run games in Chicago. That bill was negotiated with none other than hit man Frank "the German" Schweihs, a man so feared even by other mobsters that they instructed their loved ones not to hesitate to call for help if they ever spotted him around their homes. He was known as a henchman for Joey the Clown and the Grand Avenue street crew. He and Lombardo went on the lam after the Family Secrets indictments came down but were later captured. Schweihs was arrested hiding out with a girlfriend in Berea, Kentucky, but died of natural causes before he could be tried along with his coconspirators.

In the On Leong case, the former president Yu Lip Moy testified he set up one meeting with Schweihs through a gangster in Pittsburgh, saying, "I told him I wanted to come down to talk about our problem I had with Italian people in Chicago," according to the article then newspaperman John Gorman wrote on the case for the *Chicago Tribune*.

Angelo LaPietra had originally wanted to run his Italian American club on Twenty-Sixth Street as a gambling den as well, with LaMantia in charge, according to court records, but he later decided to use it for meetings instead. By 1986 it was not only being bugged and having its phones tapped but was under regular surveillance, with FBI agents noting who was coming and going as they watched. It had been raided at least once, according to one court filing, with LaMantia and another man seen trying to dispose of slips of water-soluble paper. Some of the slips were recovered, however, and they carried the results of wagers and were saved as evidence.

Investigators also continued interviewing confidential sources, who were giving up the goods on LaMantia and the Italian American club. One said he knew that characters including LaMantia, James LaPietra, Nick "the Stick" LoCoco, and Chicago alderman Fred Roti met there to discuss business and that it was a drop location for money from illegal activity. There were several phones there, the source told the feds, including one private line used to discuss juice loans and gambling. That's the one the feds targeted for their wiretap.

Another source told investigators he often took part in a craps game run by mobsters on the club's second floor. Federal authorities noted in their paperwork that another potential witness, identified as "Eric Smith," had linked that second man and LaMantia to a dice game held near the Hungry Hound Restaurant.

At the time, the innocuously named Mr. Smith also was deep into other work for the government, an effort that would tear a hole in the fabric of how Chicago thought about its court system. But all that would be revealed later.

Meanwhile, during 1986 and '87, federal records show that the taping effort had extended to a phone line at the LaMantia home on South Shields, the same residence where Martha DiCaro had been shot a half decade earlier. Angelo LaPietra's house in Berwyn also was targeted, and the effort was richly successful. The federal government captured more than a thousand calls going to and from the homes and the club, they reported in court papers, including more than two hundred allegedly involving Shorty LaMantia.

In one recorded telephone call from Angelo LaPietra to the club, he talked about a "captains meeting" to occur there on a Tuesday night, May 5, 1987. The FBI agent who wrote an affidavit on the matter stated that it was apparent from the conversation that LaMantia and James LaPietra ran the meeting and that the gatherings occurred on a regular basis. In the September 2, 1987, affidavit, a confidential source was quoted as stating that meetings took place at the club for the purpose of discussing Outfit business and were attended by organized crime members and associates. He stated that those normally in attendance included James LaPietra and Shorty LaMantia.

What was captured on federal recordings were snippets of players in the organization chattering on about the minutiae of running a gambling ring:

Did ya, did you get it?
    I got 'em, delivered 'em, I got to go collect now. I'd like to grab Yooko. He still owes me, that son of a bitch.
    Well, why didn't ya?
    Where am I going to get him? Is he working tonight?
    Yes.
    Maybe I'll stop in after I drop you off.

It was a morass of jabbering about who owed who what and who would be collecting it and who wanted to put more on which basketball game or horse race, but investigators were able to piece things together.

Some of the messages were clearer:

You tell him, we want ours and I don't give two fucks what you do, tell him that other guy is going to come see ya and he'll want this motherfucker the next day, you do what you have to . . . you are too fuckin' nice to him in his fucking car you know how much money he owes us. You tell this fuckin' Jew ain't nobody could ever be, be more replaceable. Have Kurt . . . knock the shit out of him. We don't get shit, I can't knock that fucking figure down, take another fuckin' year and a half. I don't understand it. Well, fuck this motherfucker.

It would take another few years for Shorty LaMantia to be indicted. But when the case hit in 1993, the Twenty-Sixth Street crew was charged as a criminal enterprise within the Chicago Outfit, in a document that outlined years of activity and read like a sweeping account of illegal gambling across Bridgeport and Chinatown. There were even references to old-school "wirerooms," where bettors could call in and get information on odds for horse racing and sports and place wagers.

"Defendant Joseph Frank LaMantia, also known as 'Shorty,' was one of the lieutenants or assistants to the boss of the enterprise," the indictment read. "In that capacity he supervised others that were in charge of various income-producing activities of the enterprise. At times he collected 'street tax' payments, resolved disputes, and received reports of accounts as to the income producing aspects of at least a portion of the enterprise."

A collection of players and associates were caught up as well, including LaMantia's stepson, Aldo Piscitelli, known on the street as "Shorty Junior." A man named Joe Wing, or "Joe Eng," supervised the day-to-day parts of the business in Chinatown, reporting to Piscitelli.

Angelo LaPietra sat at the top of the food chain of the conspiracy, which the government said went back to at least 1978. And the enterprise they laid out was Mob 101, with various elements of the business propping up other parts in a circle of crime. Gambling was at the center, supported by juice loans, which were collected on under the threat (and delivery) of violence. Different branches of the organization paid street taxes to the mob to operate at all, effectively narrowing the margins for those closest to the action. Using the organization's bookies was a bad deal to begin with, according to the feds. A loss meant losing the amount of the bet, usually taken on credit, plus 10 percent, while a win brought in just the agreed wager. The juice loans, often taken out to cover losses, cost the mob's customers 5 percent a week, or 260 percent a year.

LaMantia was the overall manager, the feds said, while Piscitelli operated like a deputy of sorts. He recruited bettors, controlled the betting lines, and used a "clearing" system to maintain records.

"This system enabled certain participants in the business to call other participants in order to obtain the bets received by the particular clerks up to that point in the day, to determine the volume of betting activity, to establish a safe location for the maintenance of the bookmaking records other than the wire room locations and to insure the continued existence of the records in the event that wirerooms destroyed the day's receipts because of law enforcement raids," the feds wrote.

Prosecutors had clearly relied on the work to make the recordings and surveil the ring in the late 1980s, as they rattled off a dozen locations where they had monitored wire rooms or where bets could otherwise be placed. Among them were LaPietra's Italian American club and the aforementioned local tavern.

The indictment included specific references to meetings that made it clear LaMantia had been watched for quite some time. "On or about July 1979, defendants Joseph Frank LaMantia and Aldo John Piscitelli, met with an individual at the corner of 26th and Princeton, Chicago, Illinois, for the purposes of recruiting said individual as a wireroom clerk" was just one example.

One man with the last name of Gallo had been brought before the grand jury and lied about the gambling, the government alleged, even including a few lines of that questioning. "There are a number of tapes from a wiretap at [the local tavern] where an individual identifying himself as Gallo . . . was placing bets and calling the man on the other end of the phone Pap or Paps, Pappy," a questioner said. Who was that?

"I don't know" was the answer.

"There are phone calls from approximately the ninth of July of '88 to the first of August 1988. You did not make any phone calls placing horse bets with anyone?"

"No sir."

Clearly not everyone was going to be eager to testify against the ring connected to the LaPietra organization, but prosecutors were going forward anyway. They also made clear they would attempt to seize proceeds from the gambling LaMantia managed, putting a price tag on it of approximately $500,000. LaMantia ultimately would not challenge the government's evidence, choosing instead to plead guilty to several of the counts against him, including racketeering and extortion, in 1996. He was sentenced to five years in prison.

In 1997, LaMantia was still listed among influential mob figures by the Chicago Crime Commission. The group put out a report that year called "The New Faces of Organized Crime," which detailed the structure of new Russian organizations and so forth. But many of the faces were clearly old. The Chicago Outfit then had three main wings divvied up by geography. LaMantia was listed on a flowchart under "additional members" in the wing that controlled the South Side and Northwest Indiana, listed just under the name of Rocco Infelise in the mob hierarchy.

"More so than any other criminal organization, the Chicago Outfit relies on protection from an 'unholy alliance' between the mob, corrupt police officers and corrupt public officials to survive and perpetuate itself. Without this cooperation, the Chicago Outfit would cease to exist," the group wrote, noting there were some seventy made members of the group at that time.

"Individuals who are identified as members of a particular crew do not necessarily know each other. They are aligned with supervisors who ultimately answer to the higher ranking members of each crew, and the leaders of The Outfit in general. Off the street operations are permissible by anyone in the organization. Any person who is paying street tax to organized crime is referred to as 'spoken for,'" the commission reported. "The Chicago Mob of 1997, like generations before them, is like a serpent that sheds its skin. Its present appearance may be different but, beneath the surface, it is the same dangerous beast."

The commission's description was prescient in some ways. It was ten years before the Family Secrets convictions gutted Outfit leadership. Some defendants in that case argued, apparently truthfully, that they didn't know other defendants who had been caught up in the same sweeping conspiracy case that attacked the mob as a criminal enterprise with independent moving parts.

Chicago organized crime figures are infamous for coming up with ailments during their court proceedings in an attempt to gain sympathy or allowances from judges, walking into court with canes or neck braces or casts that tend to disappear when they leave the courthouse. So some might have rolled their eyes in 2002 when LaMantia's lawyer, the venerable Ed Genson, filed a motion asking the court to terminate parts of LaMantia's supervised release because he had a heart condition and cancer. The heart condition was one of the main reasons he had pleaded guilty in the first place, Genson wrote, and LaMantia had grown too sick to make it to the probation office.

But in this instance, the claims of ill health appear to have been bona fide. LaMantia died just months after his request was filed.

His influence would be felt for at least a few more years. The feds raided about a dozen taverns in Bridgeport in 2009, looking to crack down on video poker machines, before they were legalized in the state. At the time the machines could be played for secret payouts from boxes of cash kept under some bars and controlled by Outfit associates.

"Authorities believe the video poker machines, which produce illegal payouts, tie back to the operation of the late Joseph 'Shorty' LaMantia, a top lieutenant in the Twenty-Sixth Street Crew, which operates in Bridgeport and Chinatown," Chicago's NBC 5 News reported in the wake of the raids.

LaMantia wasn't there to see the last parts of his gambling business ebbing away. As for his son Rocky, he had his own list of problems.

At the time of the Bridgeport raids, Rocky LaMantia was in state prison. He had never reached his father's criminal status, but his name, if nothing else, kept him on the Outfit's periphery in the minds of some investigators. He had at times slipped into a life of crime, though perhaps without the "organized" part.

In 1995 he was arrested for possession of a firearm, a file that drew special attention from Sherlock because he wanted to know: What firearm? The gun used to shoot Hughes obviously was never recovered, and neither was the one used to kill Martha DiCaro, for that matter.

It was April 26, 1995, when a radio call came in about a man with a pistol in the 2900 block of South Federal. When police rolled up, a juvenile appeared and said a guy had gone into an apartment holding a weapon. The cops knocked on the door and found a man and a woman inside. The man was Rocky LaMantia, who would be arrested by the end of the encounter. His occupation in the paper-work was listed as "truck driver."

The officers explained why they had been called there, according to a police report, and the woman told them the gun was in a suitcase, pointing to it.

"[Officers] removed the gun from the suitcase and unloaded it," the report states. "The owner of the apartment told officers that the arrestee entered the apartment with the gun and told her to put it up for him."

But nowhere in the report did the officers note the make and model of the gun, which is what Sherlock was looking for. Could it have been a .32 revolver—the kind of weapon believed to have been used in both the Hughes and DiCaro murders? There was no record of the confiscated gun anywhere else either, and the pistol was probably destroyed.

Later in 1995 LaMantia was arrested for driving around the West Side impersonating a police officer with an accomplice. The pair would act like they were making arrests and then rob those they took into "custody." LaMantia apparently needed the money, filing for personal bankruptcy the same year, at age thirty-six.

LaMantia's robbery scheme made the *Chicago Sun-Times*. "Marquette District patrol officers arrested the two about 7:30 PM May 23 after they spotted a gray 1987 Lincoln two-door traveling in reverse in the 3100 block of West Roosevelt Road and pulled it over," the paper reported a detective commander saying. They had an eighteen-year-old in the back of the car who told police he'd been robbed of cash. LaMantia served a year of home confinement.

Years later, LaMantia was back in the paper, this time linked to the scandal-plagued Hired Truck Program. *Sun-Times* reporters Tim Novak and Steve Warmbir had exposed fraud in the program in a series of stories dubbed "Clout on Wheels." The upshot was that city hall was hiring private companies to provide dump trucks for city jobs at hourly rates. Perhaps not surprisingly, some of the companies had mob ties, many of the companies appeared to be making campaign donations to get in and stay in the program, and lots of trucks were sitting around doing nothing. Much of the contract money was flowing to companies linked to the Eleventh Ward, which includes Bridgeport. LaMantia's Dialex Trucking reportedly made more than $400,000.

Federal authorities were all over the scam, and charges soon followed. The ensuing scandal was politically damaging to then mayor Richard M. Daley, who had placed reputed mob bookie Nick "the Stick" LoCoco—who also had been linked to Shorty LaMantia's club—in charge of the program as an employee of the Department of Transportation. LoCoco was charged with secretly owning a truck that made money off of the program, but he died in a fall from a horse in 2004 before he could be tried. That sounds like a euphemism, like the time Frank the German was recorded telling an associate that someone had gone to open a hot dog stand in Alaska, but it was apparently true. A fire official in the town where it happened told the *Tribune* the horse had stopped suddenly and LoCoco didn't.

Dialex Trucking eventually disbanded, but years later, state records still listed a onetime company officer with the same last name as Aldo "Shorty Junior" Piscitelli, and an address at what had been the LaMantia home on South Shields.

Three years later in the summer of 2007, more bad press. Reporters noticed the jowly Rocky LaMantia hanging out at the Family Secrets trial, sometimes in the courtroom and sometimes in the hallway. He wasn't a defendant; he told some onlookers he was researching a book. But instead of writing it, he was arrested that fall for taking part in the robbery of a pawn shop on Roosevelt Road, a ramp away from the Dan Ryan Expressway in the South Loop.

According to a police report on the incident, officers responded to a robbery in progress at ABBA Jewelry and Pawn after three African American men started a smash-and-grab there in a day-time raid, reportedly using hammers to break the tops of glass cases. A fourth guy, who was White, stood to the side as if he was a random customer. Workers there told police that was LaMantia, who was apparently a regular. He was gone by the time the police arrived, as were the robbers, who seemed to have fled in a white Jeep, the workers said.

The big plan started to come apart when responding officers spoke to a man who worked behind the pawn shop as a parking attendant. He had been behind the store when one White guy and three Black guys in a white Jeep pulled up and started to leave the vehicle in the wrong spot. The driver, the White guy, handed him five bucks and said they wouldn't be long, according to police documents.

Next thing the attendant knew, the place was being flooded with squad cars, and he heard about the robbery from employees, who told him about the three Black guys.

"Was there a White guy with them?" he said. "An Italian?"

While police were still there, LaMantia returned—in the same vehicle, police reported, which probably wasn't the wisest of moves. He started to tell police he had been inside when the robbery went down, and now he was back to see if everyone was OK. They were, but the parking attendant was still there and pointed Rocky out.

Police searched the Jeep and found "numerous items of jewelry matching items taken in the robbery and still bearing the victim business tags." LaMantia was arrested.

In the police lockup, he pleaded his case, according to notes of detectives who spoke to him. He was at a nearby shoe store, LaMantia claimed, when he went to the pawn shop to pick up a few things. "Rocco said that there were 2 or 3 black guys inside when he got there," a detective wrote. "The next thing he knew they were smashing up the place and taking jewelry. Rocco said that one guy had a hatchet and that he thought they were going to kill him."

LaMantia told officers he left to find an uncle of his who was a cop, but when he couldn't, he circled back to the store to check on everyone.

"Rocco was then asked about the jewelry recovered from the back of his Jeep and after a short pause related that he had picked up the pieces of jewelry when the offenders were smashing out the cases."

That version of events apparently was not good enough. LaMantia was told he would be spending the night there while prosecutors talked to more witnesses. "You have more witnesses?" LaMantia asked, according to police reports. "I don't give a fuck. I'm not going down for those three n——s."

But the police pressure did change the score a little bit for LaMantia, who adjusted his story and told investigators he never should have picked up those "shitheads," but that he could take officers to where they lived.

"He said that he was at the Dearborn Projects and ran into the three of them," police noted. "They thought he was a cop until he told them it was him, Rocco. Rocco has recently lost 150 pounds."

They had asked for a ride to Roosevelt, LaMantia said. He agreed and parked behind the pawn shop. By the time he went in, they were already inside.

"Rocco said he had no idea what they were going to do, that they just jumped up on the counters and started smashing the place with hammers and one had a hatchet," a detective wrote.

LaMantia later hired as his lawyer Joe "the Shark" Lopez, who had represented mob hit man Frank Calabrese Sr. during the Family Secrets trial that had so fixated LaMantia just a few months earlier. But his protests eventually gave way to a guilty plea, and he was sentenced to six years in prison.

He was eventually released, but Sherlock would never get the chance to ask him where he was in the early morning hours of May 15, 1976, the night Hughes was killed. There would be no chance to discuss the DiCaro murder either. Sherlock would have been eager to bear down on the particulars of that crime, to use his interviewing skills to find inconsistencies and maybe to press LaMantia about the gun. Sherlock believed it may very well have been the same weapon from the Hughes shooting.

But Rocco "Rocky" LaMantia died in 2017, at age fifty-eight, before Sherlock even took up the case. To Sherlock, LaMantia was mostly a name in piles of police reports.

According to his obituary, services were held at a simple Catholic church just a few blocks from the house on Shields. LaMantia had spent his life in the orbit of mobsters. He was buried at Queen of Heaven Cemetery in Hillside, known for being the final resting place of Chicago gangsters like his father Shorty, Tony Accardo, and Al Capone.

10

THE LAST GREYLORD JUDGE

Few single words in Chicago history resonate with the echoes of corruption like "Greylord," conjuring a dark time when the tentacles of organized crime and greed crossed what many had assumed was an impenetrable barrier no one would dare try to breach.

Named for "the curly wigs worn by British judges," according to the FBI, Operation Greylord was a deep cut into the Cook County criminal justice system—or what passed for a justice system in the 1980s. What federal investigators found, using informants and secret recording devices, was a virtual shadow-court network in which judicial decisions allowing some to get out of criminal cases—including felonies—were being bought and sold as a commodity. Eventually, more than ninety people would be indicted, including a shocking seventeen judges and forty-eight lawyers, along with a host of court clerks, police officers, and sheriff's deputies and one state legislator.

When younger Chicagoans think of "Greylord" today, however, they often commingle a series of federal undercover efforts and cases that targeted corruption in the judicial system. That includes the later Operation Gambat, a name that is the shortened version of "gambling attorney," which was a probe that snared another one-time judge, a state senator, and Fred Roti, the Chicago alderman at least one federal witness had placed at Shorty LaMantia's club. That investigation included allegations that murder cases had been fixed.

The "attorney" in that operation's name was the "Eric Smith" from the case against LaMantia and the Outfit. He was government mole Robert Cooley, considered by some to be one of the most corrupt lawyers in the history of Chicago. He was bald and had an affinity for hats and oversized sunglasses, which added to his mystique. He was a bit of a contradiction, having started his work life as a Chicago police officer, like his father and two grandfathers before him. In fact, both of his grandfathers were killed in the line of duty. Whatever his motivations for drifting toward the criminal world, Cooley eventually outfoxed everyone, escaping the system that made him by cuddling up to the government.

Prosecutors eventually credited him for helping to bring down the crooked network he once worked with. When corrupt deals were discussed at the infamous "Booth One" at the Counsellors Row restaurant near city hall, no one knew Cooley was helping the government. A busboy eventually inadvertently found a hidden camera the FBI was using to watch the table.

Cooley's efforts included wearing a wire, capturing himself delivering cash to fix court cases. Roti, whose father was a member of the Capone organization, eventually was convicted of racketeering and bribery for allegedly helping to fix cases involving mob figures. Pasquale "Pat" Marcy was accused by Cooley of having tremendous power behind the scenes in the old First Ward, which then included downtown Chicago, and in reality over much of city government. Marcy's official squishy title was secretary of the First Ward Democratic Organization, but the feds believed he was in fact a made member of the mob who did its bidding at city hall and the courts. The federal investigation against Roti and Marcy went as far as producing a bogus civil case for them to "fix" without knowing the entire matter was a government construct.

When Cooley volunteered to help the feds in 1986, just a few years after indictments in Greylord began to break, one of the tales he described for his handlers was a case Marcy was later accused of fixing. Harry Aleman, perhaps the mob's most feared hit man in his day, was blamed for numerous gangland killings in Chicago, including the 1972 murder of a Teamsters official named William Logan in his West Side neighborhood. Aleman had shotgunned Logan out of a car window in front of an eyewitness, Bob Lowe, a neighbor of Logan's who had been out walking his dog, Ginger.

Cooley told the government he once had been summoned to Counsellors Row when the topic was Aleman, who was being represented by none other than Thomas Maloney.

"Marcy asked Cooley whether he had someone to take care of a murder case involving Harry Aleman," prosecutors wrote in one filing. "Cooley told Marcy that he would check. At that time Aleman was charged with murder in a case pending before Judge Frank Wilson in the Circuit Court of Cook County. Aleman was represented in the case by Maloney at the time of the above-described conversation. After the Counsellors Row conversation, Cooley talked with Judge Wilson approximately three times about the Aleman case. Judge Wilson eventually agreed to accept $10,000 to fix the case. Judge Wilson told Cooley, however, that he wanted Maloney off of the case because Maloney had previously filed a motion for substitution of judges in which Maloney listed Judge Wilson as a judge who would be prejudiced against him."

Wilson thought it would look weird if Maloney stayed on the case and then took a bench trial in front of a judge he'd SOJ'd, so Maloney stepped aside. Prosecutors said Cooley later met up with Aleman, who, after telling Cooley he'd better be right about the case going well for him, told Cooley he could trust Maloney, and that Maloney was going to be made a judge. Which of course proved to be true.

Cooley's promise that the case would be fixed also proved to be true. Even with Lowe's eyewitness testimony.

Two veteran journalists described the case in their gripping 2001 book *Everybody Pays: Two Men, One Murder and the Price of Truth*. The tale by Maurice Possley, now a writer and researcher for the National Registry of Exonerations, and the *Chicago Tribune*'s inimitable Rick Kogan, should be on more Chicago classics lists.

Deeply sourced on the remarkable story, Possley and Kogan described how Lowe saw a car Aleman was a passenger in move by him and watched as someone yelled for Logan to come to the car after Logan exited his home. Two shotgun blasts lifted Logan off the street as Lowe looked on in horror.

Possley and Kogan described how Aleman eventually was indicted on Lowe's identification, and how his lawyer, Maloney, filed his motion to switch judges and block Wilson from getting it. When Wilson did get the case and Maloney backed away, the authors recounted a conversation between the lawyer and a prosecutor who said that was too bad, that he had been looking to go up against Maloney in front of a jury.

Maloney laughed. "What makes you think there's ever going to be a jury trial?" the authors quoted Maloney as saying.

Aleman waived his right to a trial by jury as the proceedings were about to begin in 1977, and he was acquitted by Wilson in a bench trial. The judge's stunning decision raised eyebrows all over Chicago—some of which belonged to federal investigators. The Aleman trial was credited by many as lighting a fire under the investigation that would become Operation Greylord in the first place.

Cooley told investigators he personally delivered the $10,000 to Wilson, who would commit suicide before facing charges.

Cooley's version of events has weight, considering Maloney became a judge shortly after leaving the Aleman case, and one of the cases he presided over was the trial of three New York gang members for a 1981 killing in Chicago's Chinatown, in the First Ward. The feds alleged Maloney's acquittal of those men was the result of a fix, and charged Roti and Marcy with taking in some $75,000 for their roles. Cooley testified he got $25,000. Popping up again in that case was the On Leong Chinese Merchants Association; the group acknowledged it was behind the bribe to fix the case when it pleaded guilty in its own racketeering and gambling case in 1994.

Maloney would remain a judge until leaving the bench in 1990. But if he thought he could lay low, he was wrong. A federal grand jury indicted him for bribery a year later, in 1991, and he was formally accused of fixing three murder cases, becoming the first Cook County judge to face that accusation.

One of the cases, from 1982, he reduced to manslaughter, and there was the Chinatown gang murder case in which he acquitted the trio from the New York kill squad. But perhaps most spectacular was the allegation that he fixed a case against two ranking members of the Chicago's then powerful El Rukn street gang.

The organization, which operated under the guise of a religious group, was once so influential its leaders, including supreme boss Jeff Fort, were convicted of conspiring with officials from Libya to commit terrorist acts inside the US in exchange for cash. And it was violent, known for not hesitating when it came to taking out its enemies, which were many. It was one of the first supergangs in Chicago during the period, acting almost like a corporation in structure.

Two members of the El Rukns had been charged in 1986 with the murders of two members of another large Chicago gang, the Gangster Disciples, from a division known as the Goon Squad, which Fort had targeted for moving in on El Rukn turf. The charged El Rukns were Nathson Fields and Earl Hawkins, a reputed "general." Cooley, already working for the government, had taped a fellow lawyer in a bathroom at the criminal courts building at Twenty-Sixth and California named William Swano. Maloney had taken $10,000 from Swano a full three years after Operation Greylord went public, and maybe he thought better of it. Whatever the reason, he had given the money back before the El Rukn trial, believing federal agents could be onto him. Cooley's bathroom recording captured Swano asking Cooley what was the worst thing that could happen to someone and then providing his own answer: a judge taking a bribe from you and then giving the cash back. Maloney apparently swung hard the other way, at least for appearances, convicting the men of murder and sentencing them to death.

Swano contended the gang had given him $10,000 for the original Goon Squad acquittals, saying so at Maloney's trial. He claimed that Maloney had handed it back to him at the door to his chambers after he sensed the trial was getting too much publicity and learned the El Rukns were under federal scrutiny. Cooley testified as well, of course, walking the jury through the mechanics of the payoffs. Maloney was found guilty in April 1993.

The former judge would be sentenced the following year, with Cooley again stepping up to detail accusations against him, including that while Maloney was still a lawyer, he had gone to Pat Marcy to solicit the high-profile Aleman acquittal. Aleman would go on to be convicted at a unique second trial on the very same charges, being reindicted on the theory that double jeopardy wasn't a factor because the case was fixed. After making legal history, Aleman was given essentially a life sentence of more than one hundred years and died in prison in 2010 at age seventy-one.

Cooley went on at length in his testimony against Maloney, adding more allegations against the crooked judge. This time he alleged that a 1983 double-murder trial of mobster Anthony "the Ant" Spilotro, which Maloney had presided over, was fixed as well.

Maloney had found Spilotro not guilty of what had come to be known in mob lore as the "M&M Murders." Two very unfortunate thieves had been targeted for death by the Chicago Outfit: Billy McCarthy and Jimmy Miraglia. McCarthy and Miraglia— "M&M"—had apparently been involved in three unsanctioned murders, big Outfit no-nos, and Spilotro was the enforcer tapped to get rid of them. The mob caught up to McCarthy first. His head was placed in a vise and tightened until he gave up the location of the other "M." Both eventually turned up in the trunk of a car, and the use of the vise contributed to Spilotro's later reputation as a maniacal crazy person even among his mob cohorts.

Strangely enough, the Maloney acquittal didn't turn out as a net positive for Spilotro. If he had been convicted for M&M and imprisoned, he probably wouldn't have been in harm's way a few years later in 1986. That year Spilotro was summoned home from Las Vegas, where he had been spearheading the Outfit's operations. Spilotro's criminal activity out west had made too much noise, as it turned out, so he was marked for elimination with extreme prejudice by bosses at home base who were tired of his antics making the news and bringing heat to their lucrative Vegas outpost. He was lured to a suburban Chicago basement on the pretext of being made a capo in the organization and was there beaten to death along with his brother Michael, who was falsely promised he was going to become a made guy. It was possible neither brother was completely surprised. Michael seemed to have sensed something was up, leaving his jewelry behind at his Oak Park home in the suburbs in case things went south. The bodies of the pair would be found in an Indiana cornfield by a farmer checking his plantings.

The government originally had sought to bring in evidence of the Spilotro fix before Maloney's trial, but a federal judge kept it out of the proceedings. Prosecutors had detailed the allegation in a sealed motion, saying Cooley had discussed it in a meeting about the case in another Counsellors Row rendezvous. "At some point in 1983 during the pendency of Spilotro's case, Robert Cooley, at that time a Chicago-based practicing attorney, was in the Counsellors Row Restaurant in Chicago and saw" Spilotro there as well, prosecutors wrote. Spilotro went into the back with Pasquale Marcy. "Spilotro and Marcy were gone between approximately five to ten minutes. When they returned, Cooley observed that Spilotro appeared to be upset. Spilotro then began a conversation with other persons in the restaurant besides Marcy. At some point, Cooley walked over to where Marcy was seated in the restaurant and stated to Marcy that Spilotro appeared nervous. Marcy told Cooley that Spilotro had a case up with the same guy that Cooley had had a problem with but that Spilotro had nothing to worry about because he [Marcy] had taken care of it."

But it was something else in the sealed motion that caught Sherlock's attention, something many who knew about Hughes had heard about over the years. Another case, and another alleged bribe.

It was the case against Rocky LaMantia for the murder of Martha DiCaro.

In their sealed motion, prosecutors alleged that a relative of police sergeant Sam "David" Cuomo—who had been involved in the Hughes investigation—had learned something from LaMantia about the case and trial. It wasn't clear whether the information was gathered in some kind of recording operation at, say, Garibaldi's, or whether the relative had come forward with it. But there it was, in black and white. "Shortly after Maloney became involved in the case, [the relative] saw LaMantia in a bar. LaMantia told [him] that he was not worried about his case because LaMantia's father, Shorty, was paying Maloney $20,000 for an acquittal," the motion said.

"Maloney had represented Shorty LaMantia in a number of matters before Maloney was appointed to the bench," the document continued. "Later, in a separate conversation, LaMantia told [the relative] that two weeks after the case was assigned to Maloney his [LaMantia's] father met with Maloney in Maloney's chambers at approximately 7:00 in the evening and paid him $20,000 in cash."

The motion wasn't supposed to be for public consumption, but some of what it contained wound up in the news media. It's not known whether that revelation might have been some consolation to DiCaro's family—to know that some of those who had denied them fair process in court, Maloney especially, had been snared for corrupting the system that was supposed to bring justice.

To Sherlock, it was a big piece of the circumstantial puzzle he was putting together. Shorty LaMantia had seemingly been adept at bribing law enforcement—even a judge—to keep his son out of trouble. The federal government had memorialized it in a court filing. It was certainly possible that in an era when the Chicago Outfit was meddling in law enforcement left and right, be it working with cops on the take to look the other way or something more sinister, Shorty LaMantia knew how to protect his boy.

The Maloney jury never heard about the DiCaro case. The judge had limited what the government could present in an attempt to keep the trial fair and focused on the matter at hand. But not getting information about other bribes ultimately meant little in the case against the crooked judge. He was convicted and sentenced to fifteen years in prison, despite a long speech at his sentencing hearing in which he declared Cooley to be a "corrupt, inept slob" and rambled against others who had been part of the case against him.

The pugnacious Maloney, a boxer in his youth, was obstinate to the end. At age seventy-four he testified in Chicago at a hearing for two men whose triple-murder cases he had heard as a judge and sentenced to death. The defendants, William Bracy and Roger Collins, were looking to cast doubt on their convictions and get a new punishment by showing Maloney's various problems. In an appeal of their case, lawyers pointed out that Bracy and Collins's trial came just after the infamous Chinatown trial and before another Maloney was convicted of fixing, and argued that he made an example of them to cover his tracks and preserve his reputation as a law-and-order judge. Lawyers for the pair also made much of all the information that showed Maloney was corrupt, including in his handling of Rocky LaMantia. They noted that, in files they received during their appeal, there was an allegation that a prosecutor of LaMantia had been told by a cousin of Martha DiCaro's that Maloney had been paid off, yet another indication the trial of Rocky LaMantia for the murder of the teen was fixed.

At the hearing Maloney denied ever having taken bribes, period, despite all the evidence against him. That included the government having shown jurors how Maloney repeatedly purchased money orders with cash during the years he was a judge. It didn't faze him. "Every case I ever heard was decided on the facts and law," Maloney was quoted as saying by the *Tribune* at the hearing.

Maloney died in 2008 of kidney failure at age eighty-three, not long after finishing his prison term. He remained the only judge in the history of Cook County to be convicted of fixing murder cases.

It was becoming clear to Sherlock that Rocky LaMantia had very likely shot Martha DiCaro, with a gun that was similar—if not identical—to the one that had been used to shoot John Hughes just a few years before. That gun had been made to disappear in the minutes before police arrived at the LaMantia home, where they found Shorty LaMantia promising that his son was innocent. The claim had not held up, but it didn't matter. Federal prosecutors had gathered evidence that showed the trial that followed probably was a sham, presided over by a crooked judge. Rocky LaMantia, who was so central to the Hughes case in Sherlock's mind, had skated through and been acquitted. He had never been retried based on any allegation the case was fixed.

But if LaMantia was guilty of the DiCaro murder, it certainly made him capable of killing Hughes. If you could pull the trigger on a pistol and fire a shot into the head of the girl you supposedly loved in the kitchen of your own home, Sherlock reasoned, you could certainly fire a shot out of a car in the dark at a guy you wanted to beat up.

It was sad to think that if justice had been served in the Hughes case, DiCaro might have been a grandmother by the time Sherlock picked up the investigation, he thought. More determined than ever to do something about it, he turned his attention again to the best clue he had.

11

A GREEN CHEVROLET

Rocky LaMantia and Judge Maloney weren't the first things on Sherlock's mind when he knocked on the door near Midway Airport in November 2018. He was concentrating hard on what he had to do in that moment. In fact, he was so tied up in his thoughts that he would forget the day of the visit happened to be his wedding anniversary. The case was occupying every corner of his mind.

He had decided to move forward, in part because of how credible Mary Mestrovic Murrihy had been. Very, very credible, he thought, and he had told his FBI bosses the same. Mary was an excellent witness, bolstered by the fact she didn't really want to talk about it at all. He had sensed no lies or embellishment in her account.

Sherlock believed his best route to cracking the Hughes murder was still the car, even though so many years had passed. He had names of people who had access to a car that matched the description of the shooting vehicle and was in the area the night of the crime, a car that had been driven out of state the night of the murder. He had found them in the few police records he managed to recover and had been able to locate them.

The family name of Paul Ferraro's girlfriend was in the reports, and after some detective work Sherlock found himself knocking on a door. It swung open, and an eighty-one-year-old woman greeted him warmly. Though the woman was a senior, she had her wits about her. She invited Sherlock inside, and for a moment he was encouraged. But it wouldn't last.

When he began by introducing himself as a CPD investigator, the woman thought Sherlock was there about her neighbor. Someone who lived near her was trying to get hired by the police department, and she had assumed Sherlock was part of a background check or something. So when Sherlock began to explain that he was there about the Hughes murder and her daughter, whose boyfriend had the green Chevy, she grew cold rather quickly. She didn't remember the killing, she told him.

But Sherlock needed to press ahead. Paul Ferraro had given his alibi as being with his girlfriend, babysitting in her neighborhood. It would have been a home almost directly across the street from this woman's home in 1976, Sherlock knew. He figured Ferraro and the woman's daughter would have broken up long ago. Surely their relationship was the stuff of high school and was ancient history. Maybe this woman would now be willing to say something about the car and why the group of them had driven it away while Hughes was still at the hospital, Sherlock thought. Maybe she would put him in touch with her daughter.

"Was that your daughter who dated Paulie Ferraro in 1976?" Sherlock asked, using a softer voice than he usually spoke with. He wanted to seem nonthreatening.

Yes, the woman told him, that was her daughter. "They went to a prom together," she said. "I've got nothing else to talk to you about."

It was best to break it off at that point, Sherlock thought. There was no need to be confrontational, and he had other routes to pursue.

It was a few weeks later that Sherlock was talking to a fellow officer from Bridgeport, the kind of guy it could be helpful to run things by when it came to the neighborhood and the history of the families there. Sherlock gave the cop a fill, describing what he had been up to, and how he had landed on the woman's front steps. He described their brief conversation.

The cop looked at him. The woman's daughter had married Paulie Ferraro, the cop said flatly.

The news took a second to sink in. Then Sherlock looked at him with wide eyes. "They're married?" Sherlock said, not trying to hide his disbelief. Another surprise in a case that was full of them. He shook his head, feeling a bit like a dad who was going to have to go scold a child for being caught in a fib.

Soon Sherlock was walking back up the steps at the house near Midway. The older woman's evasiveness was, of course, not making him any less interested in this angle. Quite the opposite.

His strategy was to confront her and come across as perturbed, but not to overdo it and badger the woman or frighten her into silence. Sherlock went over and over it. While he was angry and wanted to communicate there was some trouble, he wanted to be let into the home again. She once again opened the door.

Sherlock greeted her in a bit of a sing-song but stern tone, like you might use to get a toddler to pick up their toys. "You told me a lie the last time I was here," his voice trailing higher at the end.

"I know," she replied, somewhat sheepishly. "Come on in." She was smiling, as if she knew the jig was up. Sherlock's approach had worked. He was just disarming enough that it was clear they would have a conversation.

"You wanna tell me something about your daughter?" Sherlock said.

"Yes. They're married, they're married," the woman answered. And another thing: she remembered John Hughes being shot like it had happened yesterday. It was horrible, and it wasn't the kind of thing the neighborhood just let fade away.

Sherlock began to walk her through the scenario that had been painted in the old interviews in police reports. What did she remember about that night? Did she recall the babysitting going on across the street? Paul Ferraro had told police in 1976 that he had been there all night with her daughter, leaving only to get a sandwich.

The woman answered that she wasn't sure about it, or at least didn't remember that the two were babysitting specifically. She said she did remember driving in the car in question to Indiana, and that it was the night of the Hughes murder, but she said she didn't know what time it was.

In his mind, the moving of the car made sense, especially if someone had borrowed it and word had gotten to the the woman's family that it had been used in a crime. There was a possible connection between her family and the LaMantias, he knew, and it was very possible Rocky LaMantia had been driving the car and had shot Hughes. Warning could have come through those channels, or could have come from Nick Costello if he had been in the car and returned it. He had been picked up near the babysitting site on Emerald by other teens cruising the area. Hughes had been shot at around 1:15 AM, and Ferraro told police the car was taken to Indiana at 2 AM. It was possible everyone realized the car had to get out of Chicago. In those days many families didn't have a car, and many that did only had one. People tended to know who drove what.

Sherlock began to press. "Why? Why leave to go to the summer home at 2 AM?" Sherlock asked. Had they ever done that before?

In her memory, no, the woman answered.

"Then why that night?" Sherlock asked.

There was a pause, and she said she didn't know. If she had an answer to give beyond that, she didn't offer one. There was no excuse, no story about a sick family member or some other reason for heading out of state, seemingly suddenly. But while she provided no reason for going to Indiana at 2 AM, she said she remembered the trip had been the night of the Hughes murder.

Sherlock wanted to know, had she heard police could be looking for a car like Ferraro's? That might provide at least a more innocent explanation. Maybe she just didn't want there to be any confusion about it.

"I know it wasn't Paulie's," the woman told him, not quite answering the question Sherlock had asked. A police officer had shown up in Indiana early that day, she volunteered, meaning later on the morning of the shooting. This police officer had interviewed Paul, she went on as Sherlock asked for the details. The officer went over to the car himself, she said. One officer. He inspected the car and asked a few questions about whether anyone had borrowed it.

The scenario was a head-scratcher for Sherlock on a few levels, but he didn't interrupt.

Paul said no, no one had borrowed the car. After looking at the vehicle, the officer had announced that there didn't appear to be any damage on it, she said, and people had been saying bats were thrown at it.

Despite not remembering some key details, including the reason for leaving for Indiana at such an odd hour, the woman's memory was good on this. She said that's why she knew her son-in-law wasn't involved and that the car had been cleared. In her mind it was over, Sherlock thought.

Odd thing, though: Sherlock knew he had no report of any car being examined in Indiana. What he did have was the single-sheet report of a green Chevrolet being looked at soon after Hughes's death. The time didn't match what the woman had told him, but it apparently was the car. The criminalistics sheet, signed by detectives, said the car was photographed. Under the line for "location found," someone had written "NONE." Sherlock had placed a yellow Post-it note on the report, he remembered, and written "Where did this occur?" Maybe now he had an answer. One line of the sheet noted activity at Area Three, as if the photos had been taken there, but the woman he was speaking to said she was certain. She may have volunteered something important.

If some officers were in fact trying to help scrub this car, keep the teens involved out of trouble, and hide what happened, had they known it would have looked weird for an evidence technician to appear a state away to process the car with no accompanying notes? There were no reports showing how the car had come to anyone's attention, who had found it, and who sent someone to Indiana. The sheet simply said five photos had been taken of it, as if that was supposed to remove the car from suspicion forever. *At least now, that's not the case*, Sherlock thought to himself. Who knew whether any part of the police sheet on the 1972 Chevrolet could be trusted.

Sherlock later jotted down his thoughts in his own notes. "It would have been highly unlikely for an Evidence Technician to drive out of state without being accompanied by a detective or supervisor or both," he wrote. "In a CPD supplementary report dated 5/17/76, detectives . . . document no damage found on the vehicle and no sign the license plates were removed or replaced. No mention in the CPD reports where the inspection took place but [this woman] was adamant that the event took place in Warsaw, INDIANA."

He was an experienced Chicago police detective, to say the least. Sherlock knew no evidence technician would drive five hours outside Chicago by himself to inspect a car that was possibly involved in a homicide. Protocol would dictate that a detective and a supervisor, if they had good probable cause, would have gone, and with plenty of paperwork in tow. Or it would have been two detectives and a supervisor, more likely, and if they determined there was something to be looked at, *then* they would call for an evidence technician. None of this made sense.

And the single page filed by the tech had seemed to hinge on there being no damage to the car. The witness accounts collected at that point—and even those received decades later by Sherlock— did not agree that any bat flung toward the car had come in contact with it as it sped away from Root and Lowe. Put yourself in the shoes of an eighteen-year-old who just watched his good friend get shot in the chest and probably tried to get away himself. That teen probably isn't keeping his head long enough even to throw a bat, Sherlock thought.

Even if there was no damage, there were five photos of the car cataloged, according to the piece of paper. Where were they? The only photo of any car in the official record was the blue Nova, which had nothing to do with anything.

And the woman he was speaking to wasn't done surprising Sherlock. She said she knew Ferraro had been brought to the police station a few days after the killing, once they all returned from Indiana, and had been questioned. She told Sherlock that when she heard Paul was there, she called her "cousin" Jackie—Jack Townsend—who went to the Ninth District and brought Ferraro home. Townsend was the high-ranking police supervisor who served as Mayor Daley's security chief, and who had already been identified in the case as possibly being Nick Costello's uncle. Sherlock knew Bridgeport was insular and its families were often interwoven, and its residents typically had just a few degrees of separation from nearly everyone else there, but this was getting ridiculous. Thanks to Townsend, it seems, Ferraro had only been at the station for a few hours, given a handwritten statement, and left.

What the woman actually believed or knew about the crime itself was difficult for Sherlock to discern, but there were only a few possibilities. The first was that it was all an innocent coincidence, and no one she knew had anything to do with the murder. It was random that her daughter's boyfriend had the same car as the shooter, random that the family had an Indiana getaway planned for the middle of that night, and random that they happened to leave shortly after the fatal shot was fired.

The second was that most of the first scenario was right, but that the car was moved for a reason related to the murder. Either news had spread that police were looking for a green Chevrolet like the one Ferraro drove, and he and the woman's family had decided to take it out of the neighborhood to avoid being hassled, or they knew that Ferraro had lent the car to some troublemakers and wanted to just get the car out of the spotlight to avoid being tangled up in it. If that were true, they still should have felt obligated to report the car being loaned, Sherlock thought, but clearly that didn't happen.

But it was the third possibility that continued to play in Sherlock's mind. That version would be the most damning for this woman's family—and for Ferraro, for that matter. No one had seen Ferraro in the shooting car, and the best eyewitnesses had placed the gunman behind the wheel. That seemed unlikely to be Ferraro himself, and Sherlock's top suspect was still LaMantia. So in version three, Ferraro had loaned his car to LaMantia, Costello, or another friend who was with them. Word had come that things had gotten out of control, a shot had been fired from the car, and now the cops were looking for it. And Rocky's whereabouts were unknown in the time immediately after the shooting. What if he had gone home and told his father he was in trouble? Had Shorty LaMantia asked, or even told, this woman's family to get the car out of Chicago? The DiCaro case had shown Rocky would go to his father for help in a pinch, and that he would get it.

One step was for Sherlock to track down the cousin Ferraro and his girlfriend apparently were babysitting for. Sherlock found her, and the woman said she was, in fact, related to the girlfriend's family, and that her cousin often babysat for her during those years. She did not recall whether one of those times was the night of the shooting at Boyce Field, however.

It wasn't enough to confront Ferraro with, Sherlock thought. Maybe the teen just left his keys in the visor and often let friends know where his car was if they wanted to borrow it. He was tied up babysitting, after all, and probably having some alone time with his girlfriend. Sherlock wanted to build up to something that might provide a little leverage.

The old police reports laid out the entire scenario once a careful observer put the pieces together. When a group of teens left McGuane Park and drove toward the shooting, they naturally went down Emerald, which was a one-way south. At Thirtieth is where they said Costello was picked up, near where Ferraro would have parked his car babysitting. It's natural to think Costello, if he in fact was in the car, might have wanted to go back and see what had happened, or could have thought it would look less suspicious to appear there. In Sherlock's mind, LaMantia, if he really was the shooter, might have been more savvy and known to stay away. He wasn't with Costello when a group of teens picked him up, or when the kids in the car were stopped by police near the park a short time later.

As 2018 was turning into 2019, Sherlock found himself bouncing from rumor to rumor as he ran down his witness list. He caught up to a retired CPD detective, Michael McDermott. McDermott had been assigned to a Chicago cold-case unit in 2000, one that had briefly taken up the Hughes murder. Its work, along with attention from the Cook County state's attorney's office, had led to Costello's ex-wife, who told the grand jury and prosecutor Linas Kelecius about statements Costello had made about who was in the car.

McDermott didn't give Sherlock much to go on. The case's problems were ones he already knew. They were looking at LaMantia, but there was no physical evidence. No shell casings, no fingerprints, no gun. Everything was pointing in that direction, but it fizzled out.

Sherlock's report on speaking with one man who knew Hughes was typical. "He stated he was two years behind Hughes in high school but stated he knew Hughes well," Sherlock wrote. "He described Hughes as very smart, class president, and a very good athlete. He stated Hughes was popular in Canaryville and Bridgeport, known as a quiet, tough kid."

Word had spread quickly that LaMantia could be involved, the man told Sherlock. But in 1976, no one who cared for their own safety was accusing him of anything.

12

A SICK FEELING

Sherlock spoke to Larry Raddatz at his home in the southwest suburbs. Raddatz was the friend who had been with Hughes the night of the shooting and pretended his car wouldn't start when it looked like they might have to drive to a fight.

When Sherlock told him the case was reopened and that he was working it, Raddatz had immediately agreed to speak with him. Sherlock liked him immediately. The house was a working man's home and reminded Sherlock of his own house. It was outfitted with just the essentials, nothing more and nothing less. Just like much of the South Side, where Raddatz was from. It was a place of pride, but there was no putting on airs.

Sherlock could tell Raddatz was a particular person and one who liked order. And, in fact, he was a manager at an industrial safety company. It felt to Sherlock that they would probably run in some of the same circles, all things considered. And funnily enough, Sherlock wound up bumping into Raddatz again not long after they spoke, seated near each other at a high school wrestling tournament at Mount Carmel High School.

Sherlock was at Raddatz's house that day partly to make sure that, decades later, Raddatz still was sure of what he had seen. His name was all over the early reports as a potential key witness, and Sherlock wanted to lock down him and two other Hughes friends on their versions. For Raddatz, like so many others, the night had started on Throop at the house party. Raddatz definitely still recalled it.

The men spoke, and Raddatz took Sherlock back to those days in the old neighborhood. And the feud. The tension was always very high between his friends from Canaryville and a group from Bridgeport. Raddatz told Sherlock about the fights between the two groups, and about his own experiences, including once being beaten up when he was a child just because of the neighborhood he was from.

And the time immediately before the shooting was no different. In some ways it was worse. Raddatz remembered having a sick feeling in his stomach that something bad was going to happen.

He remembered leaving the party and that he had been the one to drive Hughes back to Boyce Field. It was only about a four-minute drive. Once they were milling around, a few other friends returned and told Raddatz and the others about the fight on Halsted. As Raddatz described the evening to Sherlock, he omitted the part about purposefully not starting his car, but the rest of the details were the same as Raddatz and others had described them before. He told Sherlock how he saw the green car approach. He said he was bad at instantly coming up with the make and model of cars. But when Sherlock showed him a photo of a Chevrolet like the one Paul Ferraro drove, Raddatz recognized it. That was just like the one he saw.

Raddatz told Sherlock the car slowly moved toward the park and then came to complete stop under a streetlight. Raddatz could still visualize it. It had stopped just a short distance from the group of his friends standing in the park. Insults were exchanged.

As he and Hughes and their friend John Russell rushed forward, Raddatz remembered seeing and recognizing Nick Costello in the passenger seat. He still remembered hearing someone yell, "Get down!" and seeing Costello slump. The shot came a few seconds later.

So Raddatz's memory of the shooting was clear, but Sherlock still wanted to test him on what he could recall about the police and their handling of the investigation. Police reports—which Sherlock was suspicious of—said Raddatz and Russell had viewed a lineup the same night as the shooting, at 3:30 AM.

There was no way that was true, Raddatz told Sherlock. It was flat-out wrong. He would have remembered going to the police station that same night as Hughes' death, even through the fog of the shock of what had taken place. To go from seeing his friend shot to staring at a group of teens who might be responsible at a police station? He clearly would remember that if it had happened. He definitely only talked to one officer the night of the shooting, he remembered, and that wasn't at a station. It was at Mercy Hospital. He didn't recall the exact substance of what had been said, but that was it. To Sherlock, the substance of what Raddatz had said to the officer wasn't even important; he was slowly taking apart what police *said* they had done at the same time he was trying to solve the Hughes case.

Raddatz did recall seeing a lineup, but it was at least two days later. And there was another problem. While he couldn't remember every detail about what took place, he told Sherlock he was one hundred percent sure he had picked out Costello. Sherlock shook his head. Now he knew that, along with the one provided by Mary Mestrovic, a second identification of Costello was missing.

Sherlock knew that in the police report that described the alleged 3:30 AM lineup, someone had attached a photo of what police contended was the lineup that Russell and Raddatz were supposed to have seen. Officers had written that neither teen picked out Costello or anyone else.

The presence of the photo was odd in and of itself. Sherlock knew from his own police work that, prior to November 2003, detectives were only required to photograph lineups that had resulted in a positive identification being made.

He showed Raddatz the photograph of the supposed negative lineup, the one with Costello wearing a bright yellow jacket. Raddatz said while he had seen Costello at the station and had told police that, this wasn't the group he had looked at. He had never seen that group or the photo before.

If that was true, it suggested again to Sherlock that whoever had tried to make the Hughes investigation go away quietly had gone one step too far, exposing their effort to put a brick on the police work. They had suppressed Raddatz's actual identification, saying he couldn't pick anyone out when he actually had. But they had included a lineup photo in the file with Costello in it.

Also odd was Raddatz's trip to the courthouse at Twenty-Sixth and California, ostensibly to give grand jury testimony. He didn't recall the date, but he told Sherlock an officer had picked him up and driven him there. Russell was there as well, he recalled, but before they were brought in, a different officer told them it was time to leave, and that officer brought them home again. It was as if CPD was working against itself even then, Sherlock thought. Had some officers kept trying to work the case, being stymied every time it was discovered what they were doing? Sherlock knew that bringing witnesses all the way to a grand jury proceeding and then having a different cop shuttle them home would have been extremely odd in any year. There was no official record of Raddatz being brought to the grand jury at all.

In short, Sherlock believed Raddatz, much as he had Mary Mestrovic. He found Raddatz to be genuine. Raddatz gave off the vibe of a boss in a blue-collar field. He spoke directly and wasn't a showman. There was no BS, and his somewhat rough demeanor commanded attention. But when he spoke about Hughes and that night in the park, there was vulnerability that was almost startling coming from such a man. He would fold his hands and lower his head, fighting tears that would come suddenly.

Sherlock had wanted to talk to Raddatz in part to make sure he hadn't had a change of heart about what had happened. Suffice it to say he hadn't. He was as steadfast as ever. Sherlock thought the emotions may have come so strongly because Raddatz was now a father himself. He knew what it would have meant to Hughes's parents to lose their child in such a way—and then getting no justice would be salt in the wound.

The Raddatz interview left Sherlock with mixed feelings. On the one hand, he had an adrenaline rush. Aside from working toward proving who killed Hughes, Sherlock was picking at what was looking more and more like a real police cover-up. It wasn't just that things were missing from the file. It was the right things to withhold if someone wanted to derail the work detectives were doing. Errant reports that helped Costello could still be found in the record, while documentation of work that would have hurt him were missing. Sherlock knew of at least two seemingly solid identifications of Costello, and instead of police using those identifications as leverage to get Costello to tell them what happened and who had pulled the trigger, it was as if they never existed.

But Sherlock was slowly coming to the realization that he had a problem. Call it his own sick feeling. Whoever had destroyed evidence in the case probably had done enough to ensure the case wouldn't wind up in front of a judge. Sherlock had scored by finding the Gorman file, but there was still plenty of paperwork that he knew would never be found. He could rebuild what he believed had happened, and he was doing so with witnesses like Raddatz—solid and believable witnesses—but that was only going to go so far.

The goal in Sherlock's mind shifted from "solve it" to "close it."

Solving it would mean holding someone responsible. And the person Sherlock believed was the best suspect, Rocky LaMantia, was dead. But charging anyone else was going to be the steepest of climbs. Even if he got someone to admit being in the car or to point the finger at a shooter, proving it at trial was unlikely. Such key missing paperwork in a cold case would likely sink it.

A good defense attorney would put Sherlock on the stand and simply ask, "Detective, are you confident you have all the reports in this case?'"

Well, no, he wasn't. In fact, the opposite was true. Sherlock was almost completely confident he *didn't* have all the evidence and reports. Even if he answered "I don't know" on the witness stand, that was reasonable doubt right there. He couldn't look the members of a jury in the eyes and tell them he knew for certain there wasn't some other name on a police report that wasn't in the record.

No one had thrown away a fingerprint or switched a DNA sample or swapped out a shell casing, but the damage was similar. Sherlock was happy he knew with confidence that reports had been dumped wholesale, but that wasn't going to get him far enough.

After the Raddatz interview, he knew Nick Costello could be the only person to tell him enough to put an administrative close on the Hughes file. It might still be possible to finalize the case and know, for example, that LaMantia or someone else had fired the fatal shot. Still, one way or the other, Sherlock determined he would give Ellen Hughes and the rest of her family as much closure as he possibly could.

I can still tell the Hughes family, "This is what happened. Now all the rumors you've been hearing for the last forty-plus years are either proved or disproved," he thought.

Sherlock caught up to John Russell the day after he interviewed Raddatz, though the meeting had taken some effort to put together. It took some convincing. Russell had been very close to Hughes as well, and he was even more emotional about what had happened. He and Hughes had a lot in common, including being leaders in student government at De La Salle. Even talking to someone as friendly as Sherlock was going to bring back some very painful memories. And Russell was even more suspicious of the police.

That's because, according to Russell, there was a point in time when they had treated him as a suspect, either legitimately or to shift attention away from others. It had started soon after the shooting. Hughes was taken to Mercy Hospital in a police wagon, Russell remembered, because it had been one of the first emergency vehicles to make it to Boyce Field. Russell accompanied Hughes inside as it raced down dark city streets. When he was told that Hughes wasn't going to make it, Russell said he punched the wall of the wagon in a rage, badly hurting his hand. His knuckles were visibly bleeding as police started trying to sort out who was who and which teen had been in which fight. The hand injury brought Russell the wrong kind of attention. He may have talked to police at the hospital, but his memories were foggy, he told Sherlock. He couldn't recall exactly what he might have said.

As for his own memory of the park, it tracked with Sherlock's other witnesses. He had started his night at the Throop party and had seen an actual fight there. He wasn't at the subsequent fracas on Halsted, but had wound up at Boyce with his and Hughes's other friends. He saw the green Chevrolet approach slowly and stop under the streetlight, just as the others said.

He too heard the insults and curses from the car, just as the others had described for Sherlock. Unlike them, however, Russell had run toward the vehicle almost directly behind Hughes, possibly giving him nearly the same view that Hughes had as he moved toward the car.

But because he was running and because of the lighting, he hadn't gotten a good look at anyone. He saw someone on the passenger side, maybe in the rear passenger seat, who he thought had a "weak moustache," and to him the person almost looked Hispanic.

"Russell stated as he was moving towards the vehicle he observed the front passenger slide down in the seat," Sherlock put in his report. "Russell stated as the passenger was in the process of sliding down he observed the arm of the driver pointing a handgun over the passenger (Russell stated he assumed it was the driver). Russell stated he never saw the face of the driver. Russell saw the weapon fire from the car then immediately saw Hughes fall to the ground."

Russell's irritation with the police kept up when they came to interview him several days later. He knew it was several days later, he said, because a couple of officers had actually appeared at his friend's wake to bring Russell back to the police station. He thought that was in poor taste, he told Sherlock, clearly still bent out of shape about it years later.

And they continued to press him, he said, to the point of having him take a lie detector test like other suspects in the case. It had come back inconclusive.

Perhaps most interesting to Sherlock, though, was that Russell also had viewed a lineup. And like Raddatz, he disputed that it had taken place the night of the killing. Russell also was in police reports in which officers claimed that he had viewed a lineup with Costello in it and picked out no one. Sherlock showed him the photo of the lineup from the reports, the one with Costello in a yellow jacket.

Russell laughed. That definitely wasn't the lineup he had seen, he told Sherlock. In fact, he always thought the lineup he was shown was weird. It had a bunch of guys in it that seemed too old to be high schoolers.

After the lineup Russell was sitting in the station for quite a while, he remembered. For so long, he felt like everyone there had forgotten about him. And some of them had, apparently. He said he started to notice that the younger-looking men who were walking around the station had been in the lineup he viewed. At least three were cops, he said, as they had put their sidearms back on.

If he had viewed the lineup in the photo it would have been ridiculous, he said, because he knew every guy in it. Even so, he said he wouldn't have identified any of them as being in the car, simply because he hadn't gotten a good enough look to be sure.

Sherlock noticed that as he was interviewing Russell, the man's prevailing emotion was anger. Beyond any high-minded sense of injustice, and beyond any shock and sadness that the intervening years might have blunted, Russell was mad. What happened to Hughes had in some ways happened to him too.

Russell told Sherlock it was only a few days after the shooting when it was pretty clear who the main people involved were, including Costello. It seemed like "half the town" knew, Russell said.

"The police can't clear a case where two or three kids drive by in a car, shoot and kill my friend?" he said to Sherlock, "No one ever paid for it."

13

HABERKORN

Commander John Haberkorn wasn't exactly shy or keeping a low profile while he was commander of the area that included Bridgeport. In fact, it was quite the opposite.

He notably took up a bit of a personal crusade against violence on television, speaking to community groups and churches and collecting signatures in an attempt to urge advertisers away from shows he thought pushed the envelope and had a negative impact on kids who might be watching. Cop shows reportedly drew special attention from the commander. Haberkorn's effort made the *Chicago Tribune* in a story by Patricia Leeds headlined POLICE COMMANDER RIPS TV VIOLENCE, UNREAL CRIME PLOTS. "The violence on television is worse than anything we encounter," Haberkorn told the paper. "If [the police] acted the way Kojak operates, we'd go to the penitentiary.

"The TV portrayals of police work are so exaggerated they paint a picture of violence most police don't encounter in an entire career, let alone in one case."

It was a public face that would run counter to allegations called in to the FBI at the end of 1976, just months after the Hughes shooting and Haberkorn's apparent insertion of himself into that investigation.

An anonymous tipster called the Bureau in Chicago and told an agent that Haberkorn was essentially on the take. Haberkorn had a "club" of sorts, the caller said, which consisted of officers close to him who collected money from certain businesses in the Ninth District and from illicit gambling operations there. Several local taverns and restaurants were allegedly involved, with a sergeant acting as a bagman. The information was specific enough and considered reliable enough for agents to start a RICO investigation.

The probe did not end in any charges against Haberkorn, but it drew Sherlock's interest for obvious reasons when he found it in FBI records. It suggested a pathway that the Outfit could have used to influence the way police handled the Hughes case. With attention being paid to Rocky LaMantia from the early stages of the investigation, had the mob taken steps to protect him? Shorty LaMantia handled gambling for the Outfit right in that geographic area, and LaMantia allegedly had gone on to prove he was not beyond bribing his son out of criminal trouble, as in the Martha DiCaro shooting. To Sherlock, it was at least worth consideration.

At the time, the FBI also had possession of an anonymous 1973 letter from a nosy landlord who had a Chicago police officer in her building. The landlord had taken some interest in the man—and taken to spying on him, apparently—because he left for work mid-morning but got home in the early afternoon, sometimes loaded with packages. The writer's interest only grew when she learned through another officer that the man was a cop and a "captain's man" from Thirty-Fifth Street who collected money for his superior. She had seen him drive home drunk, carting cases of whiskey as well. She had made inquiries, she wrote, and learned the cop had friends at the station on Mayor Richard J. Daley's block in Bridgeport.

The letter might have been written off as the ramblings of a busybody, except for the anonymous caller a few years later. The caller had said a police staffer close to Haberkorn was the accountant for the secret club that was collecting money, and called him by a name similar to that of the nosy landlord's tenant.

FBI agents were soon poking around in the world of Bridgeport-area taverns with names like the Wagon Wheel, looking for signs of cops wetting their beaks. It was an effort that would carry into 1977 and include agents catching up to work CPD already had done. The anonymous letter from the neighbor had been enough to get light surveillance up on the cop in her building in the spring of 1974. Investigators followed him to a few bars but saw no evidence of wrongdoing and closed their case.

Agents pieced together a history of Haberkorn, noting he had been named Ninth District commander two times, the first being in 1973. It was a plum job, they knew, in part because the station was so close to the mayor's home. Haberkorn had political contacts, they learned, and owned a security agency that provided guards for places including the International Amphitheatre and Comiskey Park. At least one internal affairs officer reported believing Haberkorn used "unorthodox measures" to eliminate his competition in this business. CPD also had at least one file on Haberkorn from 1971, when another officer alleged that Haberkorn would sometimes shake down tavern owners busted for serving underaged patrons. Supposedly a quick payoff would mean nothing would go on anyone's record.

The FBI investigation wound down to agents speaking to several tavern owners in 1977. The responses were hardly shocking; no owner volunteered that they had ever been approached by any police officer for payoffs, nor admitted to being aware of any other tavern owner being approached by anyone. One owner said he would sometimes take small bets on horses over the phone in his place for a few bucks a pop. Some officers stopped in for lunch. Nothing to see here.

But the investigation wasn't without its odd claims during interviews. One Chicago cop and one former one had a few things to say to FBI agents. The one who was still with the department in 1977 said he knew that Haberkorn had a reputation of being very close to Daley and that he gave preferential treatment to other officers who had political clout.

One of the tavern owners the FBI had spoken to also had a reputation as a friend of Daley's, as well as of being a bookie. It was generally known not to give him any trouble. The officer also said he had heard that a bar owner in West Beverly wanted to open a place in the middle of Bridgeport, and Haberkorn had been the one to put a brick on that.

The former officer had even more to say. That year he told agents that he knew Haberkorn from another district and that Haberkorn was in a small group of officers who would drive around waiting for bars to stay open after their licensed closing hours. They would wait to arrest the owner and then let them go for a little cash. Another time, the officer recalled, he was on a gambling raid that resulted in a number of people being brought to the station. The main operator of the card game was taken home, and the officer shared in a windfall.

But his most spectacular allegation involved a character by the cartoonish nickname of Milkwagon Joe. There was a bit of a tiff between Mr. Joe and a local bookie, and the bookie had wound up with a cut on his neck from a broken bottle.

As the story went, Haberkorn supposedly learned what had happened and made a phone call to someone to find out where Milkwagon Joe was and to arrange to get a suitable amount of money to get rid of the case. That amount wound up being a few thousand dollars, the officer told the FBI, but he didn't get a cut of the cash.

The harrowing tale of Milkwagon Joe apparently impressed no one, and the FBI made no case. The file sat open for a couple of years before being stamped CLOSED. The investigation and its conclusion happened quietly, doing no damage to the commander's career. Haberkorn left the department two years after the Hughes killing, and became the chief of police in suburban Oak Lawn, to the city's southwest.

He continued his turn through the Chicago media, though, and was even profiled in the *Tribune* in 1985. "When you cover the City of Chicago, you cover a lot of vicious people," he told the paper, explaining how he followed stickup gangs around town. A reader could almost picture him talking to the latest beat reporter with his shiny shoes up on the desk. "There's times when I miss that action, the excitement," Haberkorn said. "It got the adrenaline going."

Sherlock would have loved to ask Haberkorn about the odd handling of Nick Costello's questioning and the breaking of police protocols during the early days of the Hughes investigation. He would have asked about the allegations in the old FBI files and perhaps whether Haberkorn had ever met Shorty LaMantia.

But Haberkorn was another person who Sherlock wasn't going to be able to interview as he worked to uncover what exactly had happened in 1976. John Haberkorn died in May 2018, at age ninety-four, just weeks before Sherlock made his fateful trip to the police evidence center looking for the Hughes file.

14

THE COP

The Dunkin' Donuts sat on a wide commercial street just outside Chicago, lined on both sides with a bramble of gas stations, brake shops, and local bars. The kind of strip common in the city's denser, older suburbs, before the flat landscape widens out into newer sprawl and cul-de-sacs.

Terry Strong sat at a table with a cup of coffee. He was older but sharp and affable. He did not give off the impression of a retired Chicago police detective, until he opened his mouth and spoke. There was no nervousness about him. He settled into his chair as Journey's "Oh Sherrie" played softly in the background and customers waited in line behind him.

He joined the department as a cadet in 1967. There wasn't any real feel-good, heroic reason. He needed work and heard they were looking for policemen. It sounded interesting. "I really wasn't burning college up," Strong said.

He started out in the identification section with fingerprints before getting on the street in 1968. "The first day I ever worked alone on a squad car, I was at Forty-Eighth and Wabash, which is now the Fifty-First Street station. It was April the fourth, 1968," Strong said.

It was the date the Reverend Martin Luther King Jr. was assassinated at a hotel in Memphis, touching off rioting in dozens of cities, including Chicago.

Strong said he was working in a one-man car, meaning he had no partner with him. He had been patrolling a grid on the South Side from Forty-Third to Forty-Fifth, and from Michigan Avenue to a street that was then South Park Way—and was later named for King himself. Supervisors called the rookie back to the station as things were starting to come unglued. "Kid, don't go out again," they told him.

A few months later it was the opposite. Mayor Daley that August ordered a crackdown on mostly student protesters at the Democratic National Convention, creating a frightening spectacle on television as light-blue-helmeted cops pounded on the young demonstrators with billy clubs. For a time, a curfew was implemented for anyone under age twenty-one. Strong was still twenty and working afternoons. He liked to joke to his sergeant as it was getting dark that he better go home.

"Get in the fuckin' car" was the reply.

As his career progressed, he went to detective school, after which his first assignment was in the gambling section of the vice control division. It was fun, and the work landed in the papers.

"Gaming raiders nab 12 in N.W. Side club," the *Tribune* reported in 1974. "Arrest son of mobster in raid," the *Chicago Daily News* added. The mobster whose son was caught was Joseph "Joe Shine" Amabile, a noted Chicago Outfit lieutenant. And the game in question usually was known in Chicago by its Cuban name, "bolita," or "little ball." It was basically a racket that was also called the "Italian lottery" or "policy" in Black neighborhoods, where bettors would put money down on certain number combos before a daily drawing. Amabile ran a club in suburban Northlake that was an alleged mob hangout, and he was once reportedly linked to the killing of a bolita operator by mob flipper Ken Eto. Amabile is listed in the 1967 Congressional Record as a syndicate figure, identified with members, "fellow travelers," and "pawns that do the bidding of the mob, who break the laws and take the risks, all to insulate 'Mr. Big' and his lieutenants from the courts."

But that was a long time ago.

By the time Strong was telling his stories at Dunkin' Donuts. Amabile's grandson, "Grocery Store Joe" Amabile—who, as the nickname suggests, actually did run a food market—had been a contestant on *The Bachelorette* and *Dancing with the Stars*, where he once robotically pushed around a glittering shopping cart during a "dance" for America's amusement while wearing a bright white suit.

"My father was a police officer. My brother's a police officer, and I was raised not like that," Joe said of his family's Outfit history when interviewed by the *Tribune*'s Tracy Swartz in 2018.

Fair enough. Strong was more familiar with the older relative.

The *Sun-Times* trumpeted about another raid Strong was part of: 16 ARRESTED IN 31-SITE BOLITA SWEEP HERE. Pulitzer winner and legendary crime reporter Art Petacque wrote that one in 1973, a little more than two years before Strong made detective and caught the Hughes case in the Ninth District. Some 140 cops took part in taking down a game that made $50,000 a week, according to Petacque's piece, which carried a picture of a deputy superintendent posing with a seized pistol and cash.

After gambling, Strong was sent to Area Three homicide, a tough section for any newer detective. Strong had actually put it down as his preference. He was young and was finding that he craved the action his job brought. He wanted to work the most active areas, even if they were the most dangerous. "We had the Robert Taylor Homes and all of that stuff along State Street," he said. "We went up in those places. Usually two of us. Sometimes without handheld radios."

Many of the nearly thirty buildings in the Chicago Housing Authority complex had gone up on ninety-five acres along the

Dan Ryan Expressway in the late '50s and '60s. For decades they marked a sad entryway for people coming into the city on the busy corridor, until they eventually were demolished. Richard J. Daley built them, and Strong remembers his impression of the place when the complex slipped from being a newly constructed community into fostering social disorder and crime.

In his time there between 1968 and 1972, Strong realized the development, in many ways, had been built "to contain" African Americans. Black Chicagoans had been moving out of South Side ghettos and toward neighborhoods like Bridgeport, the Daley fiefdom. The development literally took on the look of a dam meant to bottle up African Americans east of the Ryan.

There had been promises of a new public housing utopia in the largest development of its kind in America, but Strong dealt with the reality. Some of the sixteen-story buildings had only two elevators, if they worked at all. Some of the cramped apartments had eight or ten people living in them. "The kids want to go out and play and there's no facilities for them," Strong said. "They were not a good idea from the beginning."

It was a dangerous time to be an officer in general. Strong recalled that one officer he went to high school with and had helped to train was killed in a shootout at Sixty-First and Calumet. Others he knew would lose their lives a few years later. Another officer he had gone to high school with was William Fahey, who, along with a partner, would be shot and killed after a traffic stop at Eighty-First and Morgan. That was just two blocks from where they had attended classes at Calumet High School.

Strong's parents didn't own a home, so the family had moved around some in the area. He actually graduated from Gresham, he said, which was just across from the Gresham police station. If he had known exactly what his future track was going to be, he might have been more careful choosing the company he kept. "I had friends who used to throw rocks at the squad cars just to get the police to chase them," he said, "when things got boring."

In fact, there was one kid whose father was a policeman, Strong remembered. "He would steal cars and then walk over to the station because he knew some of the policemen. And he'd pick up a daily bulletin and see if the car he stole was on the bulletin and if it was he'd leave it," Strong remembered.

Strong eventually separated himself from the local hoods and knuckleheads, of course. One thing he noticed right away was how political CPD was. Everyone was constantly jostling for promotions through internal intrigue, and there were commonly injections of actual politics into the police world. His lieutenant in homicide was none other than Joe Curtin, who eventually would touch the Hughes case. It was Curtin, Haberkorn, and Townsend who had met by themselves shortly before a call allegedly came in from Daley and Costello was released, according to the version of events former officer John Furmanek gave the FBI in 2005.

For many years Curtin was known as "Burke's guy," with Burke being Alderman Ed Burke, himself a former cop. Before Burke had a regular CPD detail, Strong said, Curtin was known to do Burke's bidding and shuttle him around the city.

Burke would go on to become one of the most powerful aldermen in Chicago history; his influence would remain well into the new century. Known for his sharp pinstripe suits and old Chicago ways, he was a throwback to the heyday of machine politics. His seat of power was his leadership of the city's finance committee, which he kept even through the administration of Mayor Rahm Emanuel. He was long rumored to be under the eye of federal authorities, but they wouldn't catch up to him until 2019, when they charged him with racketeering. Among the allegations was that a firm redeveloping Chicago's old main post office near the river needed to go through his committee in the pursuit of $100 million in assistance for their plan.

Burke was recorded by fellow alderman Danny Solis as being upset that the firm hadn't given Burke's private law firm any business. "As far as I'm concerned, they can go fuck themselves," Burke allegedly was captured saying on tape.

It's unknown what kinds of Burke stories Curtin took to the grave with him in 2010. Strong remembered Curtin in leadership as a commander, including times that he butted heads with Haberkorn. "They were enemies. We had a homicide one time at Forty-Fifth and Ashland in a plumbing store. And it turned out to be a former employee, but he killed two guys because he didn't want any witnesses," Strong said. "So we're working on the homicide and the crime lab came in, and they're doing their thing, and next thing you know the reporters show up. Well, Curtin and Haberkorn are both there because it's in the Ninth District. And they are practically elbowing each other to get on camera. It was a travesty."

Both had big egos, according to Strong. And both were politically connected. For Haberkorn to be leading the Ninth District showed a lot, Strong said. Because it was right down the street from Daley's home, it was a natural clout post; it wasn't a big secret that Haberkorn and Daley were close.

As for the FBI file on Haberkorn, which suggested some informant thought he was protecting illicit gambling operations or collecting money from taverns, Strong never saw it. He knew a Haberkorn who was aloof and political but not crooked. That didn't mean any part of it was true or false, he said, just that he wasn't aware of it.

In any event, Strong's detective work sometimes led him to the Ninth District, where he eventually worked the murder of John Hughes. Strong had been off that weekend and was working days with his partner Jack Boyle. The two of them appeared at work the Monday after the shooting and were handed the file.

"They said, 'Here, read this over, and then go over to Nine, because Haberkorn supposedly has some information on it. He wants to talk to you,'" Strong recalled. "So that's exactly what we did."

They walked in. Haberkorn met them. "He said, 'Well, we're probably gonna be able to clear this before the day is over.'"

Haberkorn told Strong and his partner to go have coffee with two plainclothes guys who had been working the case, one of which was Furmanek. Haberkorn also told him that "this kid, Costello," who was the passenger in the front seat of the car the shot was fired from, was being brought in later by his father. "And he mentioned that he had been in contact with the alderman and the alderman had arranged it," Strong said. "Which I didn't know anything about until afterwards."

The word was that Costello's family lived very near the alderman and the alderman actually was his godfather, Strong said. That was what was said, he remembered, though he couldn't prove the claim as he sat with his coffee more than forty years later.

The alderman Haberkorn mentioned that day was Michael Bilandic, the alderman for the Eleventh Ward, which included Bridgeport and, of course, the Ninth District police station where the conversation was taking place. Bilandic was a native of Bridgeport, a corporate lawyer turned politician who had been alderman there since 1969. He counted Mayor Daley as a mentor, and he had run for office in the first place at Daley's suggestion. Daley named Bilandic to the city council's finance committee and counted him as a confidant. He would be named to replace the mayor when Daley died at the end of 1976, just months after the Hughes shooting.

But that part of Bilandic's career didn't end up as he might have wanted. His political demise is now the stuff of Chicago legend. In

January 1979, as Bilandic was seeking a new term as mayor, the city was crippled by a massive blizzard. Jane Byrne, whom Bilandic had previously fired from a city commissioner post, primaried him while using the bad snow response against him and defeated him that March, ending his mayoralty. Chicago mayors from that point until today have tried to plow the city's snowflakes practically before they hit the ground, looking to avoid a similar political fate.

Bilandic later became chief justice of the Illinois Supreme Court, and he died in 2002 at age seventy-eight.

But in May 1976, Daley and Bilandic were both still in their powerful positions, and Daley—though some believed the Democratic machine he created was beginning its downward slope—remained the most powerful mayor the city had ever known. Daley had risen from Democratic precinct captain to the Illinois House of Representatives to head of the Central Committee of the Cook County Democratic Party by 1953. It was that organization that controlled the movement of jobs and other spoils of the machine. When Daley was elected Chicago's forty-eighth mayor in 1955, he did not relinquish his committee job—instead, he united all city political power under himself, further influencing the machine's ability to raise huge patronage armies of people who could do political work and be rewarded with city jobs and other perks. That ability sustained the machine and made many of the political leaders who protected it all but invincible. Daley was reelected five times, and his consolidation of power raised Bridgeport from a blue-collar working man's neighborhood to the machine's power base. In 1976 Daley would have had nearly unlimited influence over anything taking place anywhere in Chicago, but especially in Bridgeport—perhaps even a murder investigation.

Clout would come to pull strings everywhere Strong turned. "But Jack and I didn't quite understand that because we were brand new on this case," he said. "We're thinking, 'OK, you know, maybe it is his district and Haberkorn wants to do the right thing. He didn't. It just became obvious after a while, Haberkorn. This kid came in and he just absolutely stonewalled us. And my personal opinion, now, he wanted to know what we knew, and find it out."

Costello came in, Strong remembered, and denied everything. Haberkorn ran the interview. He was a commander and Strong and Boyle were detectives. He outranked them and there was nothing they could do about it. Haberkorn's questions were straightforward and very basic, Strong recalled:

"Were you in the car?"

"No."

"Are you sure? We have proof."

"It wasn't me. She's wrong. She must've been drunk."

The "she" in Costello's answers was "a girl witness" who was there and knew Costello, Strong said. She had known him her whole life and said, "That's him." And she never varied from that. The way Strong described Mary Mestrovic made it clear they had not spoken at any recent point.

Figuring out that Haberkorn was going to be inserting himself into the case and hampering their efforts, Strong said he and Boyle decided on their own to go and get Mary and take a statement from her as soon as possible, in case something worse went down with the case. They planned to take a written statement and get the account locked in. Again, Haberkorn insisted he do the interview. Mestrovic stuck to her story of seeing Costello, and the detectives prepared a statement for her.

Strong said they even decided to use a detective's trick when they did so. There were no recordings in those days. The witness statement would have to be typed. They planned to make an obvious minor error or two so they could give it to Mary and have her make any corrections. They would make the "mistakes" obvious enough that she would catch and correct them and mark her initials with a pen. Later, if she tried to retract her statement in court if someone got to her, she couldn't claim she had never read the final statement because her marks and initials would be there fixing the errors. Of course they would never need to use the corrections, because Mary would never change her account of what happened.

At one point, Strong said, Haberkorn requested that the detectives not tell their boss, Curtin, what they were up to. It was another strange request. There was no way Strong and Curtin could just disappear for six or seven hours and not fill someone in on what they were doing. They ignored the directive, Strong said.

He and Boyle pressed forward on the case and finished the Mestrovic written statement. They had it locked in. But things weren't done being weird.

"When we finished the written statement, Jack Townsend, who at one time had been the head of Daley's bodyguard detail, he walked through the front door," Strong said. "I'm not sure what his rank was then, but I was sure it was high above mine. He was at least a chief. And he said, 'Let me see the statement.'" Strong remembered it clearly. They had just finished with Mary Mestrovic in one of the Ninth District's interview rooms, which were located near the front desk. Townsend confronted them near the desk.

Naturally, Strong and Boyle gave him the statement.

"He read the statement. He walked out the front door," Strong said, which was only about fifteen feet away. The door closed behind Townsend and he turned south. "It's my belief there was only one place for him to go," Strong said, admitting that he did not watch Townsend walk the six doors down to Daley's home. "But he did come back only fifteen or twenty minutes later," Strong said. "I was not the world's greatest detective, nor the worst, but I'm pretty sure I knew where he went."

When Townsend reappeared, he handed the statement back to the detectives.

At that point, the Costello arrest technically belonged to Furmanek and his partner, Strong recalled. And that wasn't a concern for Strong in that moment, because it didn't matter who had made which arrest, as long as the case was cleared. According to Strong, when Townsend came back, he told them to take Mary to Area Three and to call for felony review.

When doing that, officers would normally get the person who was the "riding state's attorney"—essentially, whichever prosecutor from the felony review unit was working a shift to cover charging approvals when detectives were making cases. The floater assigned that day to approve felonies, in other words.

Strong and Boyle didn't have far to go to get from the Ninth District at Thirty-Fifth and Lowe to the Area at Thirty-Ninth and California—less than two miles. But when they arrived, the key state's attorney supervisor was already there with his assistant.

Strong had nothing specific to show the prosecutor did anything wrong, but could tell something was going on. "Again. Red flag," Strong said. Nothing about the case was being worked through normal channels or in the normal ways. "They were waiting for us."

Strong and Boyle ran everything by them. Strong said the prosecutors asked the detectives what they wanted to do, and his and his partner's suggestion was to give Costello immunity, put him in the grand jury, and he would say who the shooter was, otherwise he was going to jail. The prosecutors had concerns about that, Strong said, for some reason fearing that Costello might put the shooting on himself. Many accessories to crimes lie, of course, but not many lie in a way that makes things worse for them, taking blame for things they did not do. Strong said he told the attorneys that was unlikely, and if he did it, he would be lying. They had a good witness, Mary, right there in the building with them.

The guys from felony review made a decision. Nothing was going to happen that day. Costello wouldn't be going to the grand jury. Strong and Boyle were incredulous, but there wasn't exactly an appeals process.

Over time, witnesses began to dry up. Some got lawyers. Most of the statements that were collected weren't memorable. The detectives spoke to Paul Ferraro about his car, and he denied the vehicle in the shooting was his, Strong said.

Strong caught rumors at the time about a meeting in which police supervisors had told potential witnesses not to cooperate, but he was unaware whether it might have been the rendezvous at the Coral Key restaurant allegedly orchestrated by Sergeant Cuomo. He said he knew Cuomo at the time, even working with him later in his career in a different section.

"I had heard it was in some police commander's basement or something," Strong said. It was only from Sherlock that Strong said he heard about the location of the alleged meeting.

With the benefit of hindsight, the entire thing was silly to Strong, from the neighborhood feud to the killing to the unfinished investigation. He shifted in his chair at the Dunkin' Donuts as he spoke. It was clear that it was slightly annoying that, after a long police career, the case that he was asked about in retirement was the Hughes case. None of it made sense to him at the time or on the day he was speaking about it, starting with the divisions along the ethnic lines of the Bridgeport and Canaryville teens, who were mostly second-generation Americans.

"Most of them it was their grandparents that came from other countries. And the Italians and Croatians were tight. And the other kids were all Irish," Strong said. "And their parents were all, or at least a good portion of their parents, were city workers. So they all came from the same backgrounds." Many of them went to the same high school. But "when they were out of school they butted heads all the time," he said. "Like a bunch of young billy goats."

Strong said in the immediate years after the killing he would periodically pick up the file to see whether something had been missed and there was something more to do. Every now and again a tip might surface that would send him briefly back to work on the stalled investigation. The name LaMantia was whispered, he said, but talking to him was cut off by Onesto, the LaMantias' attorney, known among police officers as a mob lawyer.

Strong also had limited contact with Haberkorn after the initial moments of the case, he said, though he did once work off-duty for him as a security guard at White Sox park. There was a concert, Strong recalled, and Haberkorn was in charge, riding around on a golf cart and barking orders.

As far as Strong knew, Haberkorn made no other attempts to directly derail Strong. "He could have been going well over my head and I wouldn't have known anything about it," Strong said. No one ever came back for more of his paperwork either, though copies of everything were sent to the chief of detectives. Cases were worked until there was nothing more to do each day, and then reports were typed and sent through channels. Strong never knew the permanent file he was supposedly feeding paperwork into was lighter than it should have been. He was surprised when Sherlock told him about the missing reports.

Periodically, whenever one cold-case group or another took up the investigation in the years following, Strong said someone he knew would tell him that so-and-so wanted Terry Strong to watch out because the Hughes case was kicking up again, as if his own conduct could be called into question. Strong lost no sleep. "So what do I care? I'm living in the same house I was in when I was on the job, and they send me a check every month," Strong said.

"They know exactly where I am. If they want to come, I have no problem talking to anyone about this case."

So how long before the case really began to fade? Strong said it stayed on his mind for several years, until he left Area Three homicide in 1980 or 1981. Even before that, he said, he was contacted by special prosecutors at the Cook County state's attorney's office, when they were supposedly looking at the possibility of a police cover-up in the Hughes case.

Prosecutors said they were looking again at the police response, and Strong said they asked him and Boyle what they should do about the case. Again, Strong said, the advice he and his partner gave was that Costello should be put before a grand jury. "It's the only logical thing you can do," he said. "To not do it is ridiculous."

The threat of time in Cook County Jail could have been enough to get at the truth, Strong said. It was basic policing that never happened. He had wanted to solve it and was convinced Costello would have pointed a finger at the triggerman eventually. It might have meant Costello would need protection, but Strong said it could have been done. He wasn't overly afraid of the Outfit, having come across some of the mob's lower-level operatives from his years in the gambling section.

But as it went, one of the biggest cases Strong touched during his career went unsolved. The shooting of a teenager in a park. When Strong thought about the killing, and his work, and the investigation that never gave a family justice, he said he would think about John Hughes and about fate. "The truth is, if he hadn't turned away, he probably wouldn't have gotten killed," Strong said. "When he saw the gun, he turned to run off, and the bullet went right into his heart."

Any of a million different things could have happened that night, and the story would have ended differently. "I'm a great believer in destiny," Strong said.

Sherlock would come to rely heavily on Strong and his account as he formed his opinions on what had happened. Like so many others he spoke to, Sherlock found him to have a straightforward Chicago demeanor. There was a sensibility to him that was only magnified by his years as a street cop. He had seen something that was wrong, and he knew it.

This was a cover-up, Sherlock had thought when he spoke to Strong himself earlier. *Bingo. It's worse than I thought.*

15

A TROUBLING LEGACY

The story of the Hughes killing and the possibility that Chicago police at high levels successfully protected suspects from being blamed and prosecuted at the behest of mobsters or politicians—or both—seem outlandish in a vacuum.

Sherlock was as skeptical as anyone. And in many ways, he found himself struggling alongside the proverbial man who attempted to describe an elephant in the dark by feel. Depending on where Sherlock peeled apart the timeline, he found what appeared to be a conspiracy of a slightly different dark shape. It was hard to determine where the outline of one possibility ended and another began.

There are, of course, many good cops in the city today, and they had predecessors who did their jobs with honor and dignity in the 1970s. Sherlock knew them. Many of those Chicago police officers were his mentors, which was part of what made the Hughes case so disturbing. He knew they were good, no-nonsense cops, and he knew what they would have done in the case had they been unfettered by whatever was going on up the food chain. They would have solved it.

But as outrageous as a conspiracy in the Hughes case might sound, if it were proven beyond doubt, where would it rank among Chicago police scandals just in the last fifty years? For a Hughes conspiracy to have been successful, it would have required several police leaders to have participated or at least looked the other away, whether each cop knew the others' reasons for doing so or not. Sherlock certainly thought it possible that Chicago's political power trust might have weighed in and asked some ranking officers to keep Costello from harm, while the Chicago Outfit may have relied on its influence with others to keep LaMantia from blame. By effect, protecting Costello protected LaMantia, as it turned out. The teens could have had different protectors, even while they had a green Chevrolet in common.

The scope of police misconduct in Chicago is considered significant by many who have studied the CPD, and in some ways that scope clarifies the possible scenarios in the Hughes matter. While many of the black marks in the department's past have been miscarriages of justice committed by individual rogue officers, some have involved complicity, oversight breakdowns, or negligent missteps among leadership. Many were allowed to happen with the protection of what is known as the "code of silence," an unwritten layer of protection officers afford each other when they fail to expose misconduct. It's a code that has allowed some corrupt cops to live double lives as criminals, and others to mistreat or abuse suspects without punishment. But it has also benefited department leadership and Chicago mayors, for whom bubbling police misconduct cases can mean lost jobs or failure on election day.

In any event, the investigation of the Hughes case didn't happen in a small town with no history of police issues. The Hughes killing happened in Chicago. And it happened at a time when the department was morphing into its modern self and the seeds of some of its worst scandals may have been taking root.

Some of those scandals involve officers whose very names are now synonymous with police corruption. Others were of a smaller scale, though still devastating to those directly involved and beyond, including some that touched Canaryville and Bridgeport themselves. A few are somewhat lost to history, such as the 1989 case of two White officers who picked up a pair of Black fourteen-year-olds after a White Sox game, ostensibly for violating curfew, before insulting and hitting them. The teens were deliberately dropped off in Canaryville, where a gang of White teens chased and beat the boys. The officers were indicted but eventually found not guilty in a bench trial. The case touched off protests in the city, and the cops eventually were fired.

It would be notable to many in Chicago that the Hughes case involved a White victim, an Irish American teenager who was from the same area of the city as Mayor Richard J. Daley and whose death was investigated at a police station just steps from Daley's house. The Chicago Police Department's troubled relationship with the city's Black citizens is now well documented. If there is truth to allegations that Daley gave his blessing to CPD slowing down an investigation with a victim like Hughes, what does that suggest was possible when it came to the department "serving and pro-tecting" the minority communities that have had so much trouble trusting the police?

Major studies have pointed out the depth of the problems. One was "Crime, Corruption and Cover-Ups in the Chicago Police Department," published in January 2013 by the University of Illi-nois at Chicago's political science department, authored by John Hagedorn, Bart Kmiecik, Dick Simpson, Thomas Gradel, Melissa Mouritsen Zmuda, and David Sterrett. By analyzing decades of news reports, the group found an "embarrassingly long list" of nearly three hundred officers who were "convicted of serious crimes, such as drug dealing, beatings of civilians, destroying evi-dence, protecting mobsters, theft and murder" since 1960.

The UIC group outlined four major findings:

First, corruption has long persisted within the CPD and continues to be a serious problem. There have been 102 convictions of Chicago police since the beginning of 2000.

Second, police officers often resist reporting crimes and misconduct committed by fellow officers. The "blue code of silence," while difficult to prove, is an integral part of the department's culture and it exacerbates the corruption problems. However last November, a federal jury found that the City of Chicago and its police culture were partially responsible for Officer Anthony Abbate's brutal beating of a female bartender. After the civil trial to assess damages, the victim's attorney declared, "We proved a code of silence at every level in the Chicago Police Department."

Third, over time a large portion of police corruption has shifted from policemen aiding and abetting mobsters and organized crime to officers involved with drug dealers and street gangs. Since the year 2000, a total of 47 Chicago law enforcement officers were convicted of drug and gang related crimes. The department's war on drugs puts police officers, especially those working undercover, in dangerous situations where they must cooperate with criminals to catch criminals. These endeavors require that CPD superiors provide a high degree of leadership and oversight to keep officers on the straight and narrow.

Fourth, internal and external sources of authority, including police superintendents and Mayors, have up to now failed to provide adequate anti-corruption oversight and leadership.

William Hanhardt became a Chicago patrolman in 1953, twenty-three years before John Hughes was killed. Over his career he showed great proficiency in solving cases, with many crediting him with thinking like a criminal himself. It turned out there was a very good reason Hanhardt had that kind of ability.

Despite being suspected of links to the Chicago Outfit and other criminal rackets, Hanhardt earned nearly a dozen promotions, rising high into the ranks of the department. By 1975, the year before the Hughes killing, he was commander of CPD's Shakespeare District.

He was asked that year about his connection to two men linked to a federal investigation of the Outfit, labor racketeer Allen Dorfman and bail bondsman Irv Weiner, who had his own mob ties. The feds were investigating the corrupting of the Teamsters Pension Fund by Outfit figures including Joey "the Clown" Lombardo. Massive amounts of Teamsters money was being used to fund new casinos in Las Vegas, which the mob would quickly figure out how to skim.

The feds were in the process of taping Lombardo that year, and famously captured him threatening an attorney on the phone who Lombardo thought might be stiffing Dorfman and the Outfit on some money he owed. The attorney was older—seventy-two—but still trying to resist Lombardo on the phone. Federal prosecutors played the tape at the Family Secrets trial in 2007.

"I assure you that you will never reach seventy-three," Lombardo threatened on the call, demanding the money. At the trial Lombardo claimed that he had just been playacting like a gangster to scare the guy. "Like James Cagney," he told the jury.

But in 1979, as Lombardo was being recorded by the feds, Hanhardt was deputy superintendent in CPD, despite his rumored mob connections. When Mayor Jane Byrne named Joseph DiLeonardi acting police superintendent, DiLeonardi took the early step of demoting Hanhardt and others, saying he was trying to rid the department of leadership with links to the mob-connected First Ward, which would later play such a major role in the Greylord scandal.

Hanhardt's demotion to head of the traffic division was short-lived. When DiLeonardi's permanent replacement, Richard Brzeczek, was named, he made Hanhardt head of the criminal investigations division. After all, Hanhardt was still being lauded for his uncanny ability to tap criminal networks for useful intelligence for the department. "Hanhardt, through his use of informants, has cleared more murders than DiLeonardi, even though Hanhardt never worked in homicide," the *Tribune* quoted Brzeczek as saying. Hanhardt found himself in charge of some twelve hundred detectives.

Things did not progress as nicely for Hanhardt's friend Dorfman. In 1983, outside a suburban Lincolnwood hotel where he was meeting a friend for lunch, someone shot him seven times and left him in a pool of blood on the pavement. The feds would link Frank "the German" Schweihs to the hit, presenting evidence he was one of two gunmen involved, though he was never charged.

Interestingly, when investigators went through what Dorfman had on him, they found his small personal phone book. Inside was Hanhardt's number.

But even with those kinds of connections, authorities could put nothing on Hanhardt. He retired with honors in 1986, even though he had turned up in Las Vegas as a surprise witness for the defense in the trial of Outfit enforcer Anthony Spilotro not long beforehand.

It would take until 2000 for the federal government to catch up to Hanhardt, but when they did, the results were fairly spectacular. His thirty-one-page indictment spelled out the cold fact that Hanhardt was himself a criminal—and a good one—while also making an accounting of all the supervisory police positions he had held. Chief of detectives, chief of traffic, commander of the burglary section, deputy superintendent for the bureau of inspectional services, and district commander. An exemplary record, which basically made Hanhardt the Colonel Kurtz of police supervisors. He had gone completely off the reservation, the feds alleged, acting as the leader of a sophisticated ring of jewelry thieves that targeted traveling sellers.

The ring included a man named Guy Altobello, who owned a suburban Chicago jewelry store, and Paul "the Indian" Schiro, who was one of the Chicago Outfit's trusted representatives out west, operating in Las Vegas as well as his home base in Arizona. Though he was eventually replaced by Spilotro as the Outfit's Las Vegas watchman, Schiro also ran his own burglary operation and was once a friend and partner of Emil Vaci, a restaurant manager and head of a tour company that shuttled gamblers from Phoenix to Las Vegas. Vaci also had been a casino pit boss and became a federal witness as investigators worked to figure out the mob's skimming operations. His eventual murder by Nick Calabrese was described during the Family Secrets trial, in which Schiro was convicted and sentenced to twenty years in prison in 2009. In the Hanhardt ring, federal authorities alleged that Schiro was involved in surveilling people in the jewelry business out west and participating in heists.

According to his indictment, Hanhardt directed the gathering of information on potential targets as others in the ring followed traveling jewelry salesmen and learned their patterns. He used his police powers as well, authorities said, and personally participated in the thefts.

"He utilized certain CPD officers to do database searches of CPD and other law enforcement computers to obtain information concerning jewelry salespersons," his indictment stated. "Similarly, he caused a private investigator to conduct credit bureau database searches and other database searches to gather information concerning individuals who were traveling jewelry salespersons." Cars, homes, and hotels were surveilled as the ring looked for the most opportune moments to take watches and high-end jewelry valued in the millions of dollars.

They went as far as obtaining luggage identical to that routinely used by some salespeople and would switch it in moments when their target wasn't paying close enough attention. Their tools were numerous, according to the feds, including "locksmith tools, keymaking machines . . . automobile keys, hotel keys, key blanks, lock picks, 'slim jims,' smoke grenades, fake mustaches and fake beard, key cutting dies, wrenches and other hand tools, evasion devices, taser, cam sets, key cutters, bulletproof vests, cameras, listening devices, and key code books."

The ring would sometimes wait for salesmen to take their cars in for repairs and then stealthily have matching keys for the vehicles made. Once, in advance of a large trade show in Ohio, they managed to repeatedly distract hotel personnel to give themselves time to make copies of keys to safe-deposit boxes, which they then raided once they were stuffed with jewelry. That 1994 theft from a Hyatt netted the group jewelry, gems, and cash to the tune of more than $1.5 million.

Hanhardt eventually pleaded guilty and mentioned his police record at his sentencing hearing at the courthouse in downtown Chicago. "I still have the same amount of pride for this building and our criminal justice system," the *Tribune* quoted Hanhardt as saying.

The judge wasn't impressed and gave him a sentence of sixteen years. It was later reduced to eleven in 2004, but Hanhardt only saw a few years out from behind bars before his death in 2016 at age eighty-eight.

When John Hughes was killed, Jon Burge had been in the Chicago Police Department for six years, including four as a detective in Area Two, in the 9000 block of South Cottage Grove on the Southeast Side of Chicago. He was elevated to sergeant in 1977 and to a lieutenant overseeing detectives in 1981.

He was a US Army veteran who served in Vietnam, earning medals including the Bronze Star. He spent time as military police there and in Korea. In Chicago, he showed a real knack for "solving" crimes and getting subjects to confess, and while many believed he carried some of the interrogation techniques he developed during wartime to the streets of the city, Burge would later deny it. He would also deny systematically torturing suspects with beatings and electric shocks while at Area Two, though that was later alleged by the federal government.

His footprint on the Chicago police department remains considerable. In many ways he came to personify the wrongful conviction era in the city and the state, a woeful state of affairs that led to Governor George Ryan emptying the state's death row and Illinois abolishing the death penalty. Before Burge, many would have had a difficult time believing there were any circumstances that would lead to anyone falsely admitting to a murder they did not commit. But Burge showed that phenomenon was real, and that inflicting the kind of punishment he did on suspects could make it happen. Authorities said Burge led a close band of detectives known as "the Midnight Crew," which used the tactics to gain confessions.

But how early should those in power have suspected there was an insidious problem at Area Two?

Probably well before an avalanche of lawsuits over Burge's conduct easily topped $100 million in payouts to men—most of them Black—who claimed they were tortured into false confessions that led to years behind bars. And probably well before 1993, when Burge finally was fired after credible allegations arose in the 1980s. It took until 2008 for Burge finally to face a criminal indictment. It was at the federal level and for perjury and obstruction of justice based on lies under oath while he was testifying in depositions in the civil cases brought by those who were subjected to his treatment.

In late 2019, the FBI released from its vault files on their investigation of Burge over the years. Among the hundreds of pages made public was a transcript of a hearing in 1987 in the case of a defendant named Shadeed Mu'min, who was trying to suppress a confession he had allegedly made in a murder case. The transcript noted there were two prosecutors there, one of whom was Cook County state's attorney Richard M. Daley, who was still two years from becoming mayor. Among the witnesses were Burge, then the commander of the CPD bomb and arson unit, and Mu'min himself.

Burge testified he was leading the violent crimes unit of Area Two a couple of years earlier, on a 4 PM to midnight shift, when Mu'min was brought from the Seventh District and turned over to him for questioning about a robbery and attempted murder at a restaurant.

Burge said he only had a conversation of five or so minutes with Mu'min and didn't really see him after that because his detectives were working the case. He said he certainly didn't harm him or threaten to kill him. "I told him the reason why he was there, told him the evidence that we had against him, told him that certain statements had been made by a codefendant in the case implicating he was one of the offenders," Burge said. "Various idle chatter. Nothing to the point. No questions relative to the case."

But that wasn't the version of events Mu'min gave when he took the witness stand.

He had been pulled over by an unmarked squad car near Seventy-First and Halsted in October 1985, Mu'min testified, and officers asked him about having guns in his car. He did have a pistol in his car, he said, and he was taken in for questioning.

When he arrived at Area Two, he said, he was placed in a small room, and Burge entered and immediately handcuffed him to a wall. The hook the cuffs were attached to was so high, Mu'min testified, he was unable to sit down. Burge told him he wanted information about a robbery, which Mu'min said he had no knowledge of. So the two men went back and forth, before Mu'min testified that Burge said, "You'll talk before you leave here," and left the room. As an apparent message, Burge returned a few minutes later and tightened the cuffs and then left for about thirty minutes, before returning yet again and asking whether Mu'min was ready to talk. The tightening of the cuffs did nothing to spur a memory that Mu'min didn't have, and he again told Burge he didn't know what he was talking about.

Burge pushed him against the wall, Mu'min said, and then led him down a hallway to an office. There, Burge confronted him again, threatening to "bury" him in prison. Mu'min still had nothing to offer, at which point Burge told him police really were interested in his son. Mu'min still resisted and said he had no information, at which time he said Burge took a .44 revolver out of a desk drawer and removed all but one bullet from the cylinder. He held the gun to Mu'min's head and pulled the trigger three times.

"You're damned lucky I didn't kill you," he quoted Burge as telling him.

"Do you know of your own knowledge whether or not there were any bullets in the gun when he was pulling the trigger?" a lawyer asked Mu'min.

"One," he answered. "He took them all out except one."

"You believe there was one?" he was asked.

"I seen it with my own eyes," Mu'min answered.

"And did he snap the trigger slowly or quickly?"

"Snapped it slowly," Mu'min said. "He pulled it up, put it to my head and pulled it, snapped it and locked, turned it again and pulled it, and the third time he did it he took it away and said, 'Oh, you're not afraid, huh?' And I just looked at him."

Burge became enraged, Mu'min said, and jumped up from the desk. Nearby was a typewriter with a brown vinyl cover over it. Burge snatched that off the machine and pulled it over Mu'min's head.

"You'll fucking talk or I'll kill you," he said Burge told him. Burge and a detective then held the bag there, pinning Mu'min down.

"I tried to move my head but I couldn't move it," Mu'min testified. "Every time I moved he would move and push it, and finally I passed out."

"What effect did it have on you when he put the cover over your face?"

"Felt like I would die," Mu'min answered.

After Burge did that to him two more times, Mu'min said, he cracked. He would sign anything, he said he told the officers, he just wanted to be allowed to go. OK, Burge said, but he had a final message.

"If you tell somebody, nobody will believe you because there's no marks on you and you better sign the fucking statement when this attorney gets here tomorrow," Mu'min said Burge told him. "If you don't, you'll get it even worse than what I did to you now."

And it was not an isolated incident, according to those who later investigated Burge. A long series of defendants described similar circumstances of torture, along with having their feet and testicles beaten. One plaintiff, Andrew Wilson, alleged two Burge detectives used torture techniques on him to get him to confess in a case of the double murder of two police officers. Wilson said he was subjected to mistreatment including the detectives holding his abdomen and chest against a hot radiator.

That treatment did leave marks, and the injuries worried Superintendent Brzeczek enough to write a letter to Daley, who was still the Cook County state's attorney. But, again, nothing was done.

Daley would be sued a number of times over his role in the torture scandal but apparently testified in a deposition only one time. That testimony, in the case of a man named Alonzo Smith, never was made public. Smith alleged he was kicked and beaten with a rubber club, among other things, before he confessed to a 1993 murder, which he spent about twenty years in prison for. Smith alleged that Burge detectives Peter Dignan and John Byrne tortured him, and that other police officers and lead prosecutors, including Daley, did nothing about it.

As that case progressed in 2016, US District Court judge Amy St. Eve rejected a motion to dismiss the complaint, including against Daley, and issued a unique ruling:

> Plaintiff specifically alleges that while Defendant Daley was Mayor: (1) he did not disclose exculpatory information in his possession from the date he resigned as State's Attorney of Cook County in 1989 until he left the Mayor's office in 2011; (2) he did not intervene at any time to direct the CPD to disclose exculpatory information in its possession regarding Defendant Burge and detectives under his command; and (3) he did not direct the CPD to conduct a thorough and aggressive investigation of Defendants Burge, Byrne, Dignan, and the other detectives who tortured and abused African-American men while working under Defendant Burge's command. . . . Plaintiff also alleges that in furtherance of this conspiracy, Defendant Daley: (1) repeatedly discredited OPS findings of the systemic torture under Defendant Burge at Area 2; (2) refused to direct Defendant Martin (as CPD Superintendent) to initiate criminal investigations or

disciplinary proceedings against Defendant Burge and CPD Detectives under his command; (3) rejected advise from senior staff that the City should sue Defendant Burge rather than continue to defend him in civil proceedings despite Defendant Daley's knowledge of Defendant Burge's wrongdoing; and (4) made false public statements in July 2006 in response to a Special Prosecutor's Report. . . . These allegations sufficiently allege that Defendant Daley, as Chicago's Mayor, participated in a conspiracy to conceal evidence of police torture.

That special prosecutor determined Burge and his men coerced dozens of confessions but that too much time had passed to file any charges.

By 2016, of course, Daley was no longer mayor. He had turned the reins over to Mayor Rahm Emanuel, who would deal with his own major police scandal in due course. The city would go on to settle the Smith case for more than $5 million.

As for Burge, he was rousted from his home in Florida in late 2008 and charged federally with perjury and obstruction of justice. Prosecutors worked around issues with the statute of limitations by contending that when Burge submitted answers to lawyers for former death row inmate Madison Hobley denying participating in torture, he had perjured himself.

It was a relatively brief answer to torture allegations that Burge gave in a 2003 interrogatory that ultimately sunk him. "I have never used any techniques set forth above as a means of improper coercion of suspects while in detention or during interrogation" was his written response.

Federal prosecutors needed to prove up the torture to prove that Burge had lied about it, setting up a bit of a trial within a trial as Burge's history was laid out in federal court in 2010. Prosecutors presented evidence that Burge and detectives close to him systematically subjected suspects to physical and psychological abuse. Among the witnesses was Shadeed Mu'min, who repeated his tale of Burge holding a gun to his head and cutting off his air with a typewriter bag, twenty-three years after he had raised the allegation in his own case, in the hearing that the FBI kept a transcript of.

Burge ultimately was convicted and was sentenced to four and a half years in prison, most of which he served at a low-security federal correctional facility in North Carolina. After his release, he returned to Florida, where he settled back into retirement on his $4,000-a-month pension, which the Chicago police pension board had split over stripping from him, leaving it in place.

Burge died in 2018, his legacy as one of Chicago's most notorious police officers thenceforth memorialized in the history books—quite literally. After Mayor Emanuel issued a public apology for Burge's conduct, the city, as part of a settlement with many of his torture victims, agreed to add information about Burge and his crew to the high school curriculum in Chicago Public Schools in 2017.

Over recent decades Chicago has endured a number of scandals involving officers who crossed the line from trying to combat the city's vast drug networks to becoming a part of them. The playbook has ranged from simply taking money to allow narcotics rings to operate to actively becoming part of the game. Plainclothes narcotics officers often work closely with confidential sources to understand where larger quantities of drugs and cash are going to move. That knowledge can lead to certain temptations.

Some officers have found themselves skimming cash they were supposed to be inventorying. Others have stolen the actual narcotics and made their own drug deals on the side. Recent examples have included the crew of Jerome Finnigan, Sherlock's old friend, who shook down drug dealers and led to the disbanding of the special operations section. The debacle became known as the SOS Scandal and included Finnigan's eventual attempt to hire a hit man to kill a witness.

Officers Broderick "Big Thirsty" Jones and Corey Flagg led a group of Englewood District officers who were busted in 2005. The ring used informants to track drug movements and then interrupted the shipments. Jones and Flagg were known to wear their police stars and vests and stop vehicles on the street to make their illegal work look legitimate. They would confiscate large quantities of narcotics and then sell the take back into the drug networks.

"You and your merry band essentially raped and plundered entire areas," US District Judge Ronald Guzman said when he sentenced some of the convicted officers. The cops had sent "lethal poison" back onto the city's streets instead of protecting the residents of some of Chicago's poorest areas, and they had destroyed CPD reputation in the process. "People see and hear what goes on in these courtrooms," Guzman said, "and the next time they look at a police officer, they see you."

Jones was sentenced to twenty-five years as the ringleader of the group. Interestingly enough, leading the prosecution of that case was John Lausch, who would go on to be named US attorney in Chicago in 2017, leading more than 150 attorneys in that office.

Other examples of corruption have included rings of rogue cops that have been given now-familiar numeric labels after authorities caught on to their activities. The Austin Seven. The Marquette Ten. The Marquette District officers were convicted of taking bribes to allow dealers to operate. It was a scandal that would splash eventual Chicago police superintendent Phil Cline, as Cline was working in the area at the time and discrepancies arose over paperwork used to get approvals for searches in cases that would lead to the uncovering of the scandal. Cline was never accused of wrongdoing but invoked his Fifth Amendment rights when asked about it.

In the long list of officers who have gotten in trouble in the illicit drug trade, no one took things as far as Joseph Miedzianowski, considered by many to be the most corrupt officer the city has ever produced. Instead of just cavorting with drug dealers or taking bribes from them or robbing them, Miedzianowski ran his own Miami-to-Chicago drug enterprise with the help of street gangs, complete with drug couriers at O'Hare International Airport, stash houses, and fake identities. He led members of the ring, whom he protected and armed, and fixed their criminal cases if they got in trouble.

Miedzianowski, an Evanston native, became a Chicago police officer in 1976, just a few months after Hughes was killed. And like many rogue cops, he showed an unusual proficiency in dealing with Chicago's underworld. He worked criminal networks seemingly like no one else, showing a knack for getting guns off the street. He moved from early work in the Foster District to time on an elite anti-gangs unit, earning the nickname "Hammerin' Joe."

The 1998 charges against Miedzianowski were fairly epic. An indictment detailed how the cop—with the help of coconspirators, including a woman whom Miedzianowski had struck up a relationship with—moved cocaine from Miami to Chicago and then cash back in the other direction. Members of the conspiracy would transport the drugs to Chicago on commercial airline flights, and Miedzianowski and his girlfriend would meet the couriers at the airport and take them to various stash houses on the North Side. There the drugs would be processed into sellable cocaine.

"It was further a part of the conspiracy that defendant Joseph Jerome Miedzianowski protected the conspiracy from law enforcement activities of the Chicago Police Department by providing conspirators with identities of Chicago Police Officers acting undercover and descriptions of undercover vehicles involved in investigations," the indictment against Miedzianowski said. He had provided his ring with the names of informants as well. And in exchange for that help, gang members would give Miedzianowski the names of dealers that he could rob.

His story was chronicled in depth by veteran *Chicago Tribune* reporter Todd Lighty. Lighty laid out how things finally began to come apart for Miedzianowski in a 2003 *Tribune* story headlined FORMER COP CROSSED LINE, DESTROYED IT.

The unlikely tip-off came when an AT&T security operator called and left a message for Miedzianowski at gang crimes, wanting to talk to him about a wiretap. Miedzianowski knew he hadn't ordered one, so he called back and slyly asked if the question was about phone monitoring of a suspect ordered by him.

"Well, not necessarily . . . it has your name on the order," the operator said, according to Lighty. Miedzianowski hung up and quickly set about burning down his little empire, ordering players to get rid of evidence. He told one gang member to ditch a handgun Miedzianowski had given him for Christmas, investigators said.

FBI agents up on the phone line heard the end of their covert probe, and quickly scrambled to arrest members of the ring. Miedzianowski eventually was convicted in 2001, and after adding a threat to kill the lead federal prosecutor on his case, Brian Netols, to his resume, was sentenced to life in prison.

Miedzianowski maintained that his outrageous criminal career was overblown by prosecutors. "The Chicago Fire? Mrs. O'Leary's cow didn't do it, I did," he told Todd Lighty in a prison interview. "Am I behind anthrax? The Twin Tower attacks? What the hell didn't I do?"

He stayed out of the news for several years after that, until 2007, when his lawyer tried to get some of his seized property back from authorities. But instead of itemizing it, the attorney simply attached an inventory sheet to the request. It included gas masks, rifles, and bulletproof vests.

"You seem to be seeking a key to a Chicago Police Department vehicle?" the judge who heard the request said sarcastically at a hearing on the matter. Least shockingly, Netols opposed the idea.

The request also included some very unusual items, including two samurai swords taken from Miedzianowski, along with Nazi memorabilia from the WWII era. That included SS cufflinks, a dagger, and "one sterling silver Nazi SS death head ring signed 'Heinrich Himmler.'" Some of the non-weapon items eventually were made available to Miedzianowski's family.

In the fallout from the Miedzianowski case, two married ATF agents sued the city, alleging they were retaliated against by CPD's internal affairs division after they tried to blow the whistle on Miedzianowski's corruption. The same year Miedzianowski was trying to get his property back, the ATF couple attached to their court filings an expert report by analyst and onetime Los Angeles deputy police chief Lou Reiter. The wanted to bring Reiter into the case as they attempted to show how police leadership had allowed someone like Miedzianowski to thrive under their watch.

Reiter had a twenty-year police career, had consulted with departments across the country, and had been retained as an expert in more than one thousand cases. His findings in Chicago were stinging. The so-called "code of silence" was so entrenched in the city that police officers had no real expectation of being caught and disciplined for wrongdoing. According to Reiter's report, which was filed as part of the court docket in the case:

The failure of the Chicago Police Department to acknowledge its potential and take affirmative steps to eliminate or minimize the influence of the Code of Silence, in my opinion, is a conscious choice various Chicago Police managers and executive officers have taken and, in my opinion, represents a position of deliberate indifference by the Chicago Police Department to this disruptive issue within the agency. Any reasonable officer in the Chicago Police Department would be aware of the systemic deficiencies in the administrative investigative process and the discipline deliberative system coupled with the entrenched effect of the Code of Silence. Those officers who engage in misconduct and violate citizens' Constitutional rights would do so with the perception that their misconduct would go undiscovered or investigated in such a deficient manner or subjected to prolonged delay in adjudication that they would not be held accountable or sanctioned.

Reiter noted that the Miedzianowski prosecutor, Netols, had been deposed in the civil case and said he had seen such a situation in each of the eighteen cases he had brought against cops over his career. Phil Cline, by then the superintendent, had been deposed as well, and Reiter noted that Cline once had been Miedzianowski's supervisor. Cline apparently had seen enough problems with Miedzianowski to ban him from Area Five, but things went no further. Reiter also cited the deposition of former police superintendent Matt Rodriguez, who led the department at that point and said there was a backlog of police disciplinary cases. Rodriguez stepped away from the department in 1997 after the Austin Seven case had damaged its reputation and after the *Tribune* disclosed that Rodriguez had violated department rules against fraternizing with known felons. The paper reported Rodriguez had been longtime friends with Frank Milito, a man who pleaded guilty to mail fraud and failing to pay $300,000 in taxes on sales at a gas station he owned.

The ATF couple would win their suit against the city. And by late 2019, Miedzianowski was serving out his life term at FCI Pekin in Illinois. The case surely should have sounded a wide warning that there were flaws in the department and its command structure that would continue to allow problems and foster problem officers. But anyone who was expecting wholesale changes in the wake of the Miedzianowski case would be disappointed.

On October 20, 2014, what should have been a minor incident set in motion a series of events that would shake Chicago to its core and once again cast a spotlight on the failings of the city's police department and its command structure.

Callers rang in to 911 dispatchers at about 9:45 PM, reporting that a teen seemed to be trying to steal radios out of trucks sitting in lots near Forty-First Street and Kildare Avenue, near a collection of warehouses almost abutting the Stevenson Expressway on the city's Southwest Side. One caller had tried to confront him, but the teen allegedly swung a small pocketknife in his direction and started away from the area on foot.

The first Chicago police SUVs to arrive swerved into the area of the lots, only to have a witness point them toward Pulaski Road. The teen in dark blue jeans and a black hoodie—a seventeen-year-old named Laquan McDonald—was meandering on side streets and through parking lots away from the responding officers.

At one point one of the SUV's tried to cut him off, but the teen stabbed one of its tires with the knife, which had a blade of only a few inches, and officers backed off. Finally, Laquan moved through a Burger King parking lot and onto Pulaski. He continued with bounding steps, at times almost in a skip. He was a ward of the state being raised by a great-grandmother, and he had taken PCP that night, according to authorities, though it wouldn't account for what happened to him. Police radios in the squad cars chirped on and off as officers followed him, reported where they were, and asked that someone armed with a Taser report to the area to help stop the teen.

Officer Jason Van Dyke, a thirteen-year CPD veteran, and his partner for that night, Joseph Walsh, had been getting coffee at a 7-Eleven a few blocks to the south when the calls came in. They rocketed northward in a marked Chevy Tahoe, joining other officers swarming toward the scene. They arrived with Walsh at the wheel, turning left onto Fortieth just as Laquan was cutting through the Burger King lot to their south, onto Pulaski and back in the direction they had come from.

Walsh and Van Dyke jumped a curb and sidewalk in pursuit, aiming their squad back south on Pulaski, hooking around to the left of Laquan as he continued walking, and then left again around another SUV that had stopped in the median turn lane of the four-lane street. Walsh stopped his SUV just beyond that squad car, and Van Dyke quickly opened his door. Laquan continued walking southbound in their general direction but veered away from them, through the left lane of the street in the direction he was walking and then into the right lane, appearing as if he had every intention of continuing past the stopped squad cars on foot.

But that was not to be. Van Dyke stood aggressively on the median stripes on Pulaski and lifted his service weapon. Seconds later he was firing. The first shots spun Laquan, bending him slightly at the waist. He fell stiffly. More shots struck him. He landed on his side, facing Van Dyke, who continued shooting. Puffs of smoke and debris rose around Laquan's body as the officer emptied his pistol. Van Dyke fired all sixteen shots from his semiautomatic before another officer stepped forward and kicked the small knife out of Laquan's hand.

Almost immediately, the police messaging apparatus went into gear, as Fraternal Order of Police spokesman Pat Camden told reporters that Laquan had been a threat to the officers and that he had been shot after refusing to comply with their orders and lunging at them. E-mails later released to the media showed that notification of the fatal police shooting was moving through official channels. Early in the morning after the shooting, Mayor Rahm Emanuel's deputy chief of staff for public safety was notified by a Chicago Public Schools official that Laquan, a student at an alternative school, had been shot and killed by police.

The wagon-circling started just as quickly. Despite the chaotic scene and multi-vehicle response with officers viewing what happened from a number of vantage points, police reports generated that night were in striking agreement. Reporting officers wrote that Laquan was moving menacingly in the direction of Walsh and Van Dyke, and one contended Laquan had even tried to get up off the pavement after being felled by the hail of bullets. It was a company line that would be refuted by dashcam video from one of the responding SUVs, which showed Laquan veering toward his right as he walked, a distinct movement away from Van Dyke, an officer who had had at least twenty citizen complaints lodged against him, some of which were for excessive force. The video showed no attempt by the teen to attack with his pocketknife.

Emanuel's handpicked police superintendent, Garry McCarthy, would later say he met with top staffers at police headquarters and viewed the video just two days after the shooting. He told the *Tribune* in 2019 that he immediately knew the shooting was a criminal problem for Van Dyke and could even lead to a murder charge. Still, it took some nine days to strip Van Dyke of his police powers, though McCarthy later told the paper he recalled ordering it done sooner. McCarthy also said he chose not to review police reports in the case because he didn't want to interfere in outside reviews of it, a decision that would have left McCarthy unaware of apparent attempts by some officers on the scene to cover up the full gravity of what had happened on Pulaski Road.

It did not take city lawyers long to realize the exposure the case and the video represented to city hall. On March 16, 2015, city records showed that attorneys Michael Robbins and Jeffrey Neslund, who were representing Laquan's family, raised questions with the department of Mayor Emanuel's corporation counsel Stephen Patton, the top lawyer in Chicago government. They wrote him a letter days later describing problems with the police reports, which they contended were falsified.

"We have confirmed that the narrative summaries contained in the police reports of both police and civilian witnesses are false," they wrote. "Civilian witnesses who are alleged to have told the police that they did not see the shooting, have told us they did indeed see the shooting, and that it was unnecessary (which of course, is entirely consistent with the dash cam video). One witness whom the police reports alleged did not see the shooting, in fact told multiple police officers that he saw the shooting, and it was 'like an execution.' Civilian witnesses have told us that they were held against their will for hours, intensively questioned by detectives, during which they were repeatedly pressured by police to change their statements."

The city reached a settlement in principle with the lawyers and Laquan's family within days, still in late March of that year, agreeing to compensate them with $5 million. But it wasn't a fact the city would shout from the rooftops. The first public inkling of what was unfolding came in April, when Patton presented it to the City Council Finance Committee. The full council approved it April 15.

Both things conveniently happened *after* an April 7 runoff election between Emanuel and challenger Chuy Garcia, which Emanuel won.

The mayor contended he hadn't known the severity of the McDonald shooting until Patton briefed him in March, though city records showed numerous meetings between his staff and police leaders and between McCarthy and the mayor well before then. Emanuel also publicly claimed he didn't know there were wide discrepancies between the police reports and the dashcam video until its public release, which came much later.

For months the city resisted releasing the video, contending it would compromise criminal investigations into what had happened. The feds indeed were interested, and had gathered up video of the incident, including from the security cameras at the Burger King where Laquan had cut through the parking lot.

A lawsuit brought by independent journalist Brandon Smith eventually forced the issue. It argued the city was violating the Freedom of Information Act by refusing to release the video. Cook County judge Franklin Valderrama ordered it made public in November 2015, and the city held its breath.

The reaction was swift and intense, as the images of Van Dyke gunning down Laquan were broadcast around the world. Protests rippled across Chicago, including a virtual siege on the city's main shopping strip in the midst of the Christmas rush. That protest on Michigan Avenue included a march led by Reverend Jesse Jackson and saw protesters blocking the entrances to major stores as stunned tourists looked on and snapped photos with their cell phones. "Sixteen shots and a cover up!" became a familiar rallying cry. Emanuel slipped further into damage control. McCarthy was fired December 1 in the wake of the video's release, with the mayor calling him a distraction as the department tried to repair its relationship with Chicagoans.

But the mayor himself never quite shook the case. After first saying he didn't think a federal review of the department separate from the ongoing probe of the Laquan McDonald shooting was necessary, Emanuel flip-flopped and said he would welcome it. The US Justice Department launched one that same month, December 2015.

That review found serious systemic failures in training, use of force, and police accountability. The report noted that the department had received around thirty thousand complaints of police misconduct just in the five years before the study, but that only 2 percent were found to be credible by police oversight bodies, a rate that defied belief. From there, actual discipline was haphazard at best. In other words, officers believed they were operating with near impunity, and it showed in their actions on the street.

The Department of Justice's paper also included a short history of reform attempts in the city and a rundown of corruption cases, noting that "the Chicago Police Department has cycled in and out of the national consciousness almost since its inception, and the last several decades have been no exception." Modern reform attempts dated to 1972, four years before the Hughes case, when Mayor Richard J. Daley established a reform panel that took four days of public comment on abuses. Daley's son, the mayor Richard M., had his own version: in 1997, in response to the Austin Seven case, he established the Commission on Police Integrity, a panel that also was tasked with finding the causes of corruption.

Often in Chicago, such blue-ribbon panels are set up by politicians as a publicity move—a way of looking as if they are doing something about a problem or a major case. The groups are designed not to have teeth, and not much happens in response to their findings. Some are established with the intent of not digging too deeply into an issue and coming up with findings that are friendly to the politician who set panel members up in their influential posts in the first place. But that wasn't what happened with the Rahm Emanuel version of the reform panel he set up after the McDonald killing. His Police Accountability Task Force's findings were just about as damning as the federal report.

"We arrived at this point in part because of racism. We arrived at this point because of a mentality in CPD that the ends justify the means. We arrived at this point because of a failure to make accountability a core value and imperative within CPD. We arrived at this point because of a significant underinvestment in human capital," the group wrote. Its makeup included former federal prosecutors, including lawyer Lori Lightfoot, and the city's inspector general, Joseph Ferguson.

"CPD has missed opportunities to make accountability an organizational priority. Currently, neither the non-disciplinary interventions available nor the disciplinary system are functioning. The public has lost faith in the oversight system. Every stage of investigations and discipline is plagued by serious structural and procedural flaws that make real accountability nearly impossible," they wrote.

Van Dyke ultimately was charged in a state case with first-degree murder. It was believed he was the first officer in decades to face that charge for an on-duty incident. He was convicted of second-degree murder and sixteen counts of aggravated battery—one for each shot he fired into Laquan McDonald. His sentence was eighty-one months in prison, with a chance at probation after two years in custody. Ferguson, the inspector general, ultimately found in his own report that sixteen officers had been involved in the cover-up of Van Dyke's conduct. Despite that large number, which included supervisors and ten officers who Ferguson found had made false statements about what happened, just three had faced criminal charges of conspiracy and obstruction of justice. The trio, which included Van Dyke's partner that night, Joseph Walsh, were acquitted in a bench trial.

CPD itself wound up subjected to a federal consent decree, approved by a judge in January 2019, which set court-mandated goals for reforms. In late 2019, a monitor found the department had missed most of the first fifty deadlines it faced to make changes.

Ultimately, Rahm Emanuel's political career in Chicago was buffeted too badly by the turbulence of the Laquan McDonald shooting. It had a severe impact on his credibility and standing in Chicago's African American community, a key part of the coalition he needed to stay in office. Although some advisers were convinced he could still win, Emanuel announced he would not seek reelection in 2018. "This has been the job of a lifetime, but it is not a job for a lifetime" is how Emanuel explained it, not pointing to the case as a leading factor. His announcement, however, came just a day before the start of jury selection in Van Dyke's murder trial.

His successor would be task force member Lori Lightfoot, whose platform unsurprisingly included police reform. But, again, a Chicago leader found building momentum tough. She initially kept Superintendent Eddie Johnson, a department insider Emanuel had tapped to replace McCarthy. She eventually fired Johnson, however, saying she learned he had lied to her about an incident in which he was found asleep behind the wheel of his car, apparently after a night of drinking with a subordinate he was supposedly in a relationship with.

In 2019 Lightfoot became the latest in a long line of Chicago mayors to suggest the department had reached a turning point toward reform. "That must start at the top," Lightfoot said as she announced Johnson's dismissal. "That hard but important work is impossible without strong leadership focused on integrity, honesty, legitimacy, and accountability."

16

A FINAL PUSH

Despite Terry Strong's insistence that he would have no problem talking to anyone about his work in the Hughes case, he had been leery of talking to Sherlock. The two of them went back and forth a few times before Strong finally agreed to sit down with the latest person who claimed to be starting the investigation anew and considering whether the police purposefully scuttled it back in 1976.

Sherlock wasn't surprised by the resistance. It wasn't that he believed Strong had done anything wrong, it was just that he knew Strong was a "typical '70s dick," the shorthand for detective. Sherlock knew they just weren't very loose-lipped as a class, and wouldn't eagerly come forward and talk about older cases. But he also knew that if he could get Strong to talk to him, it would help to explain a lot of what he had learned.

"They don't forget names and places. They're good. They're old school," Sherlock said later. It turned out Strong knew Sherlock's uncle Bill, who was an evidence tech in CPD from that era.

Strong was quick to say that ninety-nine percent of the police officers working the case were doing the right thing, they just didn't know at the time what they were up against. The frontline cops didn't understand that when they took a step forward in the investigation, somebody behind the scenes "was taking it out, was changing it, changing its path," he told Sherlock.

Strong suggested that the first person to realize the case was going to be a problem had been his partner, Jack Boyle, who was deceased by the time of Strong's meeting with Sherlock. Boyle was the older and more experienced of the two men. Almost as soon as the two got the case, Boyle could tell what was probably coming. He had told Strong, "Watch this."

Boyle had seen a thing or two, and any murder with potential political and mob connections was bound to be a shit show. Sure enough, Strong wasn't disappointed.

Strong took Sherlock through the early hours of his getting the Hughes case on May 17, 1976, including how Haberkorn told him and Boyle not to inform his commanding officer, Curtin, what he was working on and how Bilandic had been involved in Costello being brought to the Ninth District.

Haberkorn directed Strong and Boyle to have coffee with John Furmanek and his partner. When the four men returned, Strong told Sherlock, Nick Costello and his father, a Chicago fire lieutenant, were in Haberkorn's office, and Haberkorn told Strong that he, Haberkorn, would conduct the interview.

"Strong observed Haberkorn question Costello about his involvement in the shooting death of Hughes. Costello stated he had no knowledge of the incident and refused to answer any more questions," Sherlock wrote in his FBI report. "Strong felt the questioning of Costello was fruitless."

Afterward, Strong said, he and his partner made their own plans to get Mary Mestrovic from school and bring her to the Ninth District for questioning. That was because they were "perplexed" why she hadn't already given a handwritten statement. When they arrived at the district, Haberkorn elbowed into their work again, but the two detectives still managed to prepare a written statement from Mestrovic.

Sherlock memorialized the next key portions of his conversation with Strong in what is known as an FBI 302—interview notes for the official case file. It read this way:

> When the handwritten statement was completed and signed by Mestrovic and her mother, Chicago Police Deputy Chief John Townsend, who Strong did not expect to see in the 009th District, was waiting for Strong and Boyle directly outside the office from where they took the statement. Townsend said to Strong "give me that report." Strong stated Townsend took the handwritten statement out of his hands and started to read the report. When Townsend finished reading the statement, Strong observed Townsend walk out the front door of the 009th District, with the statement in his possession, and walk south on Lowe Street heading directly to Mayor Richard J. Daley's house. Strong stated it was common knowledge that the Mayor lived down the street from the 009th District Station on 35th and Lowe. Strong stated after approximately 30 minutes, Townsend returned to the station and ordered Strong to notify felony review and to move the investigation to Area 3.

Strong, Boyle, Furmanek, Furmanek's partner, Mary Mestrovic, and her mother Rita were all taken to Area Three, Strong told Sherlock. Strong said he was greeted there by a top supervising prosecutor—another surprise to the investigators. Someone had notified him before Strong had contacted felony review.

Strong said he immediately took a moment to speak with the ranking prosecutor to discuss where they were. Sherlock memorialized what Strong told him next as his 302 continued:

> Strong stated [the supervisory prosecutor] and his partner . . . stepped away from Strong while they discussed the

case. Strong stated that the witness, Mestrovic, and her mother, were standing within earshot of [the prosecutor]. Strong stated he could hear [him] talking loudly, discrediting [Mary] as being drunk the night in question and not a reliable witness. Strong stated he believed the loud discrediting conversation between [the prosecutor] and his partner was staged. Strong noticed Mestrovic was crying and quickly became uncomfortable with her position.

When Strong told [the prosecutor] he believed he had enough to charge Costello, or at least enough to hold him for more questioning, [the prosecutor] responded defiantly, "no."

Strong stated approximately one year after his interview of Costello and Mestrovic, a Cook County state's attorney from Special Prosecution (name unknown) contacted Strong questioning why he didn't pursue the case against Costello. Strong stated he told the state's attorney to check with the boss of felony review. Strong stated that was the last he heard from the State's Attorney's office concerning the Hughes case.

Sherlock was interviewing a cop who was there, and one that he trusted. He believed Strong was telling him the truth.

Strong was clear about his theory of the case and about what his old-school plan of attack would have and should have been. Costello was the key. Attack that. He was in the car, and that was the angle to take. That had been ripped out from under the detectives with their hands on the case.

For the case to take the turn that it took had gotten Strong very upset. Strong had said as much, but Sherlock could sense the depth of the outrage. There was a family out there that had lost a seventeen-year-old son. He was here one day and gone the next. It had been Strong's duty to solve the case, and he believed he had simply not been allowed to. The intensification of the Hughes family's grief was in some ways on Strong's shoulders because of what had happened, and he didn't like it one bit. Strong was adamant about whose fault it was. This wasn't the scuttling of an investigation by a bunch of cooperating players. It was a few people at the top, the ones who had the capability to pull strings and make things go away.

Sherlock already had Jack Townsend's name in his ear at the time Strong told him the story, because the mother of Ferraro's girlfriend had told him her "cousin," whom she called Jackie, had gotten Paulie Ferraro out of the police station.

Townsend was a big and powerful man, Sherlock knew. Everyone in CPD at the time and in 2019 knew he had been Richard J. Daley's right hand. "Everyone knew, you cross John Townsend, you're getting dumped," Sherlock would recall later.

Mary Mestrovic Murrihy already had told Sherlock about her experience at Area Three, with prosecutors doubting her and making her cry. Strong had corroborated it without speaking to Mary in all those intervening years. In fact he had the habit of calling Mary "the girl witness." He barely knew her name. Strong had basically recounted Mary's story from another seat in the room. The details were the same, down to what may have been a staged conversation about Mary being drunk, within earshot of her and her mother. Strong had watched a ranking assistant state's attorney attack a teenager who was trying to help. What was the state doing demoralizing their own witness? Strong had been told there just wasn't enough to charge the case, and that essentially had closed it.

Interestingly enough, Strong also told Sherlock he later worked in the 1990s with David Cuomo, the sergeant who was assigned to city hall at one point and who allegedly held the meeting at the Coral Key. It was a mass transit overtime detail. Strong said they, not shockingly, had at one point started talking about the Hughes case. Cuomo said he thought a relative knew who killed Hughes, Strong remembered, and called him in front of Strong. That relative had an "answer" that Cuomo passed along.

"Cuomo told Strong that 'SEDAVICH' (sp?) killed Hughes," Sherlock wrote, noting the name may have been a final red herring. "Strong stated he was not familiar with this name during his time of being involved in the investigation."

At around the same time in early 2019, Sherlock was able to locate Costello's ex, who had appeared before a grand jury in 2000 and told Assistant State's Attorney Linas Kelecius what her then husband had told her about the Hughes killing.

He went to speak to her at her neat apartment—where it was very noticeable that literally nothing seemed out of place. Sherlock found her to be smart and independent. She spoke about Costello with little or no emotion. *I can't tell if she loves him or hates him,* Sherlock thought to himself.

No matter. That wasn't why Sherlock was there. He wanted to walk her through what she had said to the grand jury and make sure she still stood by it.

She did. She was married to Costello between 1981 and 1985, and he had told her he had been with LaMantia and Ferraro when Hughes was shot. The delivery was simple and factual. She was being cooperative, though Sherlock thought that she was also keeping her Bridgeport guard up.

The woman said Costello would only tell her that either LaMantia or possibly another friend had killed Hughes, refusing to specify further or provide details. But then she added something new for Sherlock that he also memorialized. She "stated, emphatically, that she knows why LaMantia killed his girlfriend, Martha DiCaro, in 1979," Sherlock wrote. "Martha and LaMantia were dating at the time of Hughes' death. Martha was also the first cousin of [the witness] and the sister of Charlie DiCaro. [The witness] stated Martha was going to tell police that LaMantia shot and killed Hughes."

The witness acknowledged she couldn't prove it, but that's what she wanted Sherlock to know. It was only at this point that she had shown any real emotion. The DiCaro family had always maintained Martha was in the process of breaking up with LaMantia when she went to his family home the day she was shot and killed, and the woman believed that one hundred percent, Sherlock thought. That much was clear. And she knew the details, too. She was quick to point out that the DiCaro gun disappeared, even though the LaMantias' official story (once the masked intruders were dismissed) was that Rocky and Martha were the only ones home.

Sherlock added the information to his growing report, also noting for the FBI record that even the transcript of the ex-wife's 2000 grand jury appearance had never made it to the official CPD paperwork. He had only found out about her from a transcript in the Gorman file. Sherlock left the apartment convinced she was telling him the truth.

Sherlock was looking for a witness who might be able to take things further; maybe Costello had let something slip to someone after the shooting, something like *I can't believe that fucker pulled the trigger.* Sherlock still needed leverage for an eventual conversation in Sandwich—or, better yet, at the Cook County state's attorney's office or at the FBI itself. He didn't envision charging anyone, but he wanted an official record to be made and for the case to be stamped CLOSED once and for all.

Sherlock interviewed more of John Hughes's friends. One was a man named John Mahoney, who had the same story as most of the others Sherlock spoke to. But he did graduate things in one interesting area.

Mahoney didn't see who was in the car, because it was too dark from his vantage point, but he was still sure he knew who two of them were: LaMantia and Costello again. He believed this because, instantly after the shooting, a number of teens who had been much closer and *had* seen the shooting said they saw LaMantia and Costello in the car. There was no question. People had seen them.

So why hadn't that been communicated more urgently just minutes later, when police officers responded to the park? Were the teens that afraid of LaMantia? Or, more insidious, had it been told to police and vanished? Had those reports gone the way of so many other reports written on the case?

Mahoney said people at Boyce Field that night immediately said they also knew LaMantia and Costello had been at McGuane Park bragging that they were going to go down to Boyce to cause trouble. Sherlock knew other witnesses had made similar statements at the time, but there was no record of the kind of chatter Mahoney was sure he had heard.

Two other witnesses, John Joiner and Brian O'Malley, told similar stories as others Sherlock had spoken to. They insisted the shooting had been touched off by the ongoing feud between the groups. Joiner told Sherlock again about the Throop party and the fight on Halsted and estimated there were some fifty people at Boyce Field when the shooting took place, Sherlock recorded.

Most important to Sherlock was asking Joiner about the police lineup. Along with Raddatz and Russell, Joiner had been mentioned in original reports as viewing a lineup with Costello in it the very night of the shooting, and police had written that Joiner did not identify him. Joiner told Sherlock he recalled being asked if he recognized a few Bridgeport kids who were standing around in a room at the station that night. They were the same guys involved in the fight on Halsted Street, Joiner said he told police, and the same who had been taken into custody after being seen near Boyce after the shooting.

But he never was asked to view any formal physical lineup and told to pick out anyone from the car or the shooter himself, Joiner said. It would have made no sense to even ask him to try. As Joiner told Sherlock, and as he told police that night, he saw Hughes after he had already been shot and after their friends had started gathering around him on the ground.

Joiner had never seen the car at all.

High on Sherlock's list to speak with was the relative of Dave Cuomo, the police officer who had run the Coral Key restaurant. Cuomo himself was by then too infirmed to speak. He was eighty-eight and would pass away just months after Sherlock caught up to the relative in February 2019. Sherlock needed the man to level with him, if he could, about what he knew. It seemed like every time Sherlock saw the man's name in the police reports, there was different information attached.

Sherlock talked to the relative at his home, which was then just a couple of blocks from the old Ninth District police station on Lowe. He had become a lawyer but had stepped away from the profession and wasn't licensed by the time Sherlock found him. Sherlock thought he appeared somewhat disheveled. But the man did have plenty to say, which Sherlock memorialized for his FBI files.

"Although [he] provided relevant information concerning the events surrounding the Hughes investigation, [he] would not divulge the source of his knowledge," he wrote. For starters, the man said he also was at the party on Throop that set the night's events in motion. He attended with seven or ten friends, he said, and was there as things started to get out of control and the fighting began. Costello and LaMantia were involved in the fight with guys from Canaryville that he didn't know. He said he wasn't in the park when Hughes was shot.

The man said he didn't find out about it until the next day when he went to the Coral Key for breakfast. Sherlock made notes and wrote out what the man said next in an FBI 302. The man told him that Cuomo, "a retired Chicago police sergeant, formerly assigned to City Hall, was having breakfast with . . . the father of Paul Ferraro, and . . . the father of Nick Costello. [He] stated he found out about the murder of Hughes by eavesdropping on [Cuomo's] conversation with Ferraro Sr. and Costello Sr.," Sherlock wrote. "[He] indicated he could not remember exactly what was said but he does recall the three men attempting to have a private conversation about the Hughes investigation."

So there was at least one living witness who had seen the Coral Key meeting.

The man put Ferraro, Lamantia, and Costello in the shooting car but would not tell Sherlock how he knew. So many years later, Sherlock thought to himself, and no one ever seemed to vary from those names. The man said it was no big secret in the neighborhood anyway, but everyone was afraid to identify them because of their various ties to powerful people. Each of the teens was related to people who could make such problems "go away," as the man phrased it. He didn't tell Sherlock who he believed had actually pulled the trigger. He would only say LaMantia was among his friends who were crazy enough and who had bragged about having guns.

"Without prompting, [he] started talking about the murder of Martha DiCaro," Sherlock wrote next. The man had just blurted it out and started talking about it, making the connection himself. Sherlock found his demeanor to be a little bit odd, but he kept going. Maybe he had some things to get off his chest, or at least figured lying to someone working for the FBI was probably a bad idea.

The man "indicated in May of 1979, LaMantia killed Martha because he feared Martha was going to break up with him and she was going to inform the police that LaMantia killed Hughes," Sherlock put in his report. The gun in the DiCaro shooting hadn't been recovered, the man knew, telling Sherlock that was no accident. In his report, Sherlock noted LaMantia had gone on to be tried in front of Judge Maloney with the known result. But the man didn't tell Sherlock about the information that the US attorney's office in Chicago had used—or tried to use—in the Maloney case. Federal prosecutors had told the judge in the Maloney case that this man knew Shorty LaMantia had paid a bribe. Whether he had told prosecutors that himself or if they had learned it another way would remain unknown.

"[He] stated 'everyone' knew LaMantia would beat the murder charge in court," Sherlock wrote in his 302. "[He] stated 'everyone' was afraid to tell the police that LaMantia was in the car that was used in the shooting death of Hughes.

"'LaMantia was untouchable.'"

17

"I REALLY WANT TO GO NOW"

Sherlock's one-man surveillance operation had to end at some point. He had periodically parked across from Nick Costello's house in Sandwich, sometimes in different cars, in the hopes of spooking him into talking. He knew Costello had seen him.

Eventually he made the phone call. When Costello picked up, he was hesitant and stuttering, Sherlock recalled later.

"Come on, Nick," Sherlock told him. "You know why I want to talk to you."

The two agreed to meet in the parking lot of a nearby restaurant. Sherlock pulled into the lot in his Cherokee, and Costello came up and got in the front seat. He was still nervous, shaking a little.

"Why are you here?" Costello asked. "Why do you want to talk to me about the case?"

Sherlock told him again that he knew the answer. It wouldn't have been good practice to get into it in the car in a parking lot in Sandwich. The goal was to drive Costello to a police station so Sherlock could memorialize anything he might say on video.

Costello knew more than he had told people about the case, Sherlock said. He tried to keep it friendly and convince Costello it

216

was ultimately going to be OK. The time had come to do the right thing.

"I don't think you're the shooter," Sherlock told him. "I don't think you did anything to harm John." Those things were true. Sherlock didn't think Costello had killed Hughes. His belief was that he was almost certainly in the car. But it was possible Costello was almost as surprised as anyone else that the shooter—perhaps LaMantia—had actually fired a gun and taken a life that night. Sherlock made a personal appeal for Costello to get whatever he wanted off his chest once and for all.

But he also had to level with him. "You don't have anything to worry about right now. You don't—now," Sherlock said. "But I am going to talk with some other people in the near future. Those people might be the people who are guilty and might be giving you up. You've seen that game before."

It was partially a bluff, mostly because LaMantia and other players in the case were dead. But Sherlock still hoped he could talk to Paul Ferraro and find out what had happened with the green Chevrolet. If Ferraro said something damaging about his car being used and Costello bringing it back to him, that could be an issue. That's where Sherlock wanted him to know things could still go.

"You know what, I really want to go now," Costello said in reply.

"Would you like to come to the police station and talk to me?" Sherlock said.

"I'll get back to you," Costello said, closing the Jeep's door.

But it was a lawyer who got back to Sherlock and his FBI partners. The state's attorney's office eventually promised Costello's lawyer there would be no charges. Authorities just wanted as good an answer as they could construct, to potentially close the Hughes case and end decades of questions.

At one point the lawyer called to say Costello was very close to talking, as long as he had assurances from prosecutors that he wouldn't be in trouble. But eventually, there was a final answer.

It was *no*. The lawyer said his client, Costello, would not be talking to them.

Nothing mattered, including immunity promises. What Costello experienced, what he may have seen, and what he may have done—none of it was going to be revealed. If Costello had spent decades trying to avoid talking about the case, that wasn't going to change for Sherlock or for anyone else.

The quiet of history tightened its grip.

Sherlock's final interview was in late 2019. He had left CPD and the FBI by then but could still collect information and pass it to his law enforcement partners. He had been hired as an investigator for the Cook County state's attorney's office, though his approach to Ferraro at that point was mostly his own doing.

Ferraro was then a member of the Chicago Fire Department and told Sherlock he would have no problem speaking with him about the case. Ferraro's position had delayed Sherlock's approach, as he wanted to have firmer information before asking about the case. But knowing time was winding down, Sherlock made the call anyway. The two met at the station Ferraro was assigned to. Sherlock knew he had little leverage, and was relying on Ferraro to simply tell him whether something had been bothering him all these years, such as someone borrowing his car, if it had been the one used in the shooting.

As the two men spoke, Sherlock found Ferraro to be very sure of himself. His demeanor reminded Sherlock of a detective on the witness stand in court. He was smart. His answers were quick and short, and he didn't carry on beyond what he was asked. There was no drifting into rambling responses.

The theory that made the most sense was the car being brought back to Ferraro and then quickly removed from Chicago. Sherlock shared with Ferraro his leading theory, that Costello had been picked up after the shooting by another car of teens on Emerald between the two parks near where Ferraro had been babysitting. Kids at the time used the street as a highway north and south, mostly staying off Halsted because of traffic and more police patrolling it.

Ferraro knew nothing of that, he said confidently, and he would never let anyone borrow his car. He had only spoken to police the one time not long after the shooting, and never had again until meeting Sherlock that day, he said. He hadn't seen Costello since 1976, Ferraro said, and didn't even recall exactly how he had learned of the Hughes shooting.

So what about the quick trip to Indiana? That was planned, Ferraro said.

So, when had he left? Sherlock asked. "No later than midnight," Ferraro answered.

Well, Sherlock said, when Ferraro had talked to police last, he told them it was about 2 AM. It was obviously an important point, as midnight was before the Hughes shooting and 2 AM was after. Maybe it was early morning, Ferraro said when challenged on the point, but police had looked at his car anyway. Whatever car had been used in the killing had been damaged, Ferraro said. There was nothing linking his car to the crime.

Sherlock hadn't known exactly what to expect, and had mostly gone to talk to the fireman to cross the final moves off of his checklist. Ferraro didn't give him anything he could use to advance his work. And there certainly hadn't been a disclosure of any long-held secret about where his car had been the night Hughes died.

The bid for a final bombshell ended. If what Ferraro had said was not truthful, it meant the wall of silence had carried forward across decades.

Sherlock knew what he would probably have to do next, and it wasn't something he was looking forward to. He would have to reach out again to John Hughes's sister Ellen, whom he had spoken to many months earlier after picking up the Hughes file. He had started his work with her blessing, and now he would have to tell her what he had—and hadn't—been able to do as he worked to solve the case of her brother's killing. There were answers he had, and some that would never come. How would she react?

Sherlock struggled with approaching Ellen. He called and he texted, but he didn't hear back. Finally he texted again, and there was a reply. "Come tomorrow," she wrote him.

Sherlock drove to Ellen's home by himself. It was December 2019. It was a lonely drive, with time to reflect on what had transpired. Christmas decorations flickered on many of the neat homes on the blocks of Canaryville and Bridgeport as he passed the local landmarks he knew well.

Ellen and her husband greeted him warmly. There was small talk about politics and their families. Sherlock started with some personal news. He was stepping away from CPD and the FBI. Obviously John's murder had not been closed in the way he wanted it to be, but there was still a glimmer of hope. Sherlock would be joining the Cook County state's attorney's office as an investigator, hopefully working cold cases. He told Ellen he would keep an eye on the case for as long as he was still working.

"I don't see what else I can do on this right now," Sherlock said. "But I definitely want to keep this file close to me."

Sherlock did not mean it as some empty thing to say in a difficult professional moment. He knew that he would keep the file close. And if someone—Costello or anyone else—ever came forward, he would be there.

"They thanked me in the Canaryville way," Sherlock said later, remembering the talk. "Their voices didn't rise any octaves. They just said, 'Thank you,' and I accepted it.

"I knew they weren't going to jump up and hug me."

Any disappointment Ellen Hughes felt was, of course, reasonable. But Sherlock had done much in the face of difficult circumstances.

He had found compelling evidence of a police cover-up. He had found serious irregularities in the handling of the Hughes case that suggested someone in authority did not want it solved.

That list of findings included proving definitively that there was paperwork missing from the official police file that should have been there. By locating the Gorman file, he found reports and notes that someone had made sure were omitted from the record. Additionally, he had found multiple witnesses who said they were brought to the main courthouse at Twenty-Sixth and California, though no records existed showing they had been there at all.

He had shown to a reasonable degree of certainty that the lineups viewed by witnesses had been manipulated. Larry Raddatz and Mary Mestrovic, who had not communicated with each other, both had testimonies inconsistent with police records. They each had been named in the reports as having viewed a lineup that contained Nick Costello and having failed to pick him out. Someone had taken the extra step of including a lineup photo that did include Costello, standing in a conspicuous spot with a bright yellow jacket. Both Raddatz and Mestrovic swore they told police they did see Costello at the police district, despite that not being recorded.

The inclusion of the photograph would have gone against police protocol in the first place, as negative lineups typically were not photographed and preserved. Someone was trying to make a point, Sherlock believed.

John Russell's account was perhaps even worse. His lineup apparently had been filled with younger-looking police officers, which he knew because he saw them milling around the station later with their guns back on their belts. Yet the official record still included not a photo of the lineup of cops but the same one with Costello in his yellow jacket, and a note that Russell did not pick him out.

Mestrovic shouldn't have been viewing a lineup at all. When a witness tells police, "I know him; I grew up with that guy," there's typically no need for one. She had already positively identified Costello, who was someone she knew, as having been at the shooting scene in the car the fatal shot was fired from. In a police report, an investigating officer should simply have written that Mestrovic had identified Costello, nickname "Horse," as being in the passenger seat, and note she had known him since fourth grade. Maybe there would be a need if she hadn't seen him for ten years, Sherlock thought, but that clearly was not the case. And not only was a lineup allegedly done, she was still recorded as having failed to positively make an identification.

Sherlock also had developed a legitimate police witness who worked the case and corroborated the irregularities. Terry Strong detailed how command-level officers had big-footed working detectives and taken over interviews—another situation that was all but unheard of. And Sherlock had learned that one of those high-ranking officers, John Haberkorn, had wound up under investigation himself for possible criminal activity, although no case was made.

And Strong's account included claims that were closely corroborated by prior testimony. Retired officer John Furmanek had gone to the FBI in 2005 with some of the same complaints, stating that Costello had been released from custody after Mayor Richard J. Daley made a call. Strong said the word in the station at the time was that Costello, on top of everything else, was a godson of Daley confidant Michael Bilandic and his father was a ranking firefighter. Strong told Sherlock that Daley's right-hand man, John Townsend, had taken interview notes from the detectives and marched them out of the Ninth District in the direction of Daley's home just before that call would have been made.

Strong also corroborated Mary's account of her being mocked and dismissed by officers who were supposed to be supervisors and then her testimony being discounted once prosecutors got involved.

Sherlock had developed a working theory of what could have happened the night Hughes died, one that included a car that matched the description of the one witnesses had seen. He had learned from another interviewee that the car had, in fact, been moved out of Chicago in the middle of the night just after the shooting.

The list of irregularities in the police work grew with the information that an evidence technician had traveled alone, out of state, to give the car a clean bill of health. A police report recording the examination of the car had failed to note that the inspection of the vehicle had taken place not in Chicago but in a neighboring state.

Sherlock had found and interviewed a relative of the policeman who ran the Coral Key restaurant. He had corroborated accounts of a meeting there that included Costello's father and police leaders who allegedly discussed the case. Strong said he had been summoned to the same restaurant to give an accounting of what was happening in the investigation, off the books, as had Furmanek before him.

Finally, Sherlock had tracked down Costello's ex-wife. She had repeated to him what she had previously testified to, about Costello placing the main suspect in the case, Rocky LaMantia, in the shooting car. And she had taken her account a step further. While it was uncorroborated, she told Sherlock she knew that Martha DiCaro, her cousin, was going to break up with LaMantia when she went to his home one day a few years after the Hughes murder. DiCaro was afraid of her boyfriend, and her family thought she was trying to end an abusive relationship. The ex-wife said she believed DiCaro had a trump card. She would tell police that LaMantia had killed Hughes if he did not leave her alone. LaMantia shot her in the face, the woman believed, and he would never face punishment for the crime because his mobster father had bribed a Greylord judge, which was something federal prosecutors also believed.

If certain police supervisors did scuttle the Hughes investigation at the behest of powerful politicians or forces from Chicago's underworld, and if LaMantia was in fact the shooter, Martha DiCaro was an unintended follow-up victim of that misconduct. But there were others who would remain affected by a failure to get justice.

They included members of the Hughes family, for whom the loss of their son and brother remains an open wound. For Ellen Hughes, it was the memory of her older sister awakening her from a cold sleep to tell her that her brother was gone, a memory that stung all the more with the knowledge that no one paid for taking him away. And it had brought fear to her parents. They weren't "a cop family," so it had taken them longer than it probably should have to realize that police weren't going to be solving the case, perhaps purposefully so. They had hired their own investigator, only to have him scurry back to their home so afraid that he would only tell them in their backyard that he had been urged to leave the murder alone.

The neighborhood itself suffered as well. What were once blocks where children and teenagers roamed freely changed overnight. Magical summer nights hanging out in darkened Chicago parks faded into memory for many youngsters in Bridgeport and Canaryville. A friend had been taken from them, but a measure of their innocence had, too. Parents were understandably unsettled. The way many viewed their neighborhood changed permanently.

For Mary Mestrovic, it was years of disillusionment. She had attempted to do the right thing for her friend, and she had done so even in the midst of threats and fears. She endured harassment from friends of the boys she believed had been involved, repeatedly being antagonized at work and followed home. She had taken the risk that police often beg and plead with witnesses to take. *Speak out. Say something, for your community and for justice.* Mary had done it for nothing.

She had gone to college, gotten married, and had a career and two kids of her own, but the case stuck with her. At times it flashed in real time. Like when LaMantia died and she started getting texts, including from her son. She had been away at school for the DiCaro murder, and it had faded from her mind. So she googled LaMantia and learned how he had been acquitted. "I was like, 'Holy cow,'" she said later. "He got away with it."

Needless to say, what happened to John Hughes would now stick with Sherlock as well.

As a police officer—and a good one—he could see the angles play out in his mind. If the case were handled properly, it would have been over in days. It was clearly solvable, despite the lack of physical evidence, such as a gun or shell casing left at the scene.

"This is not a case that should have become a cold case," is how he put it. "All night long we have a fight between kids from Bridgeport and Canaryville. It's not World War II. It's not a bunch of different countries involved. It's two groups of kids that everyone knows."

The detectives and the tactical officers who worked the streets each night, they knew them all. "Let's use the highest number. Let's say there's twenty kids from Canaryville and twenty kids from Bridgeport. They're fighting all night, it's already documented," Sherlock said. "That incident on Thirty-First and Halsted. These coppers who worked that district, they know who's out there."

The kids from Canaryville had just finished beating up the kids from Bridgeport in the street, and those teens were mad about it. Both sides retreated to their park, and a short time later, the green Chevy was heading in.

"A 1970s detective? That case is solved that night. There's no mystery," Sherlock said. "It's not a gang drive-by. It's not a robbery gone bad. These are the kids from the fight on Halsted. They came back and shot at the kids from Canaryville in Boyce Park."

Grab the right twelve kids, do the work, and the defenses come down, he said. "Rocky LaMantia's lawyer calls Area Three and says my client took a polygraph at a detective agency, and he passed, and I don't want you talking to him, and that's it?" Sherlock said. Even then, he was the most likely suspect, and all work in his direction had stopped. No one had been brave enough to say anything. "Nobody wants to be that one person."

But with his work finished, the time for theorizing was over.

"It literally bothers me," Sherlock said. He had grown to like Ellen and her family very much, and he thought he had let them down. He had started his investigation thinking maybe it could be different. Maybe he would be the one to break through and go to the Hughes family and be able to tell them what had happened, who had done it, and why. Closure.

"It upsets me now. I've had a lot of success in my career," Sherlock said, "and this is the way I'm going out. I'm leaving a case open."

It is accurate to say, though, that the Hughes case, instead of being a reflection on Sherlock's abilities, is more a reflection on his city.

Chicago was John Hughes's city, and Sherlock's, and Mestrovic's. But it was also LaMantia's, and Burge's, and Miedzianowski's.

Historically, many in positions of power in the city have grown adept at doing just the sort of thing that frustrated Sherlock and has frustrated so many others. Masking the truth. Looking out for their own interests at the expense of others and then covering their tracks.

Adding forty years to a case that seemed marred by conspiracy had left it virtually unsolvable, save a miraculous new admission by someone who may have seen something or been a part of it and never before come out of the shadows. But in many ways, Sherlock still gave the Hughes family a gift. With the kind heart of a good police officer, he cared. He recognized what they had gone through and the vacancy in their lives and tried to give them answers. Some would say he found them.

But like no other case in his years with a badge, Sherlock was pushing against the city's unmoving structural beams. He was not the first—nor will he be the last—to end his effort without getting absolute fairness and true justice.

Perhaps at least as often as anywhere else on earth, things happen in Chicago that should never happen to anyone. And what should happen—if God were keeping close watch on the dark sky-scrapers on the shore of Lake Michigan—doesn't.

Clouded. Unforgiving. Infuriating.

Chicago.

EPILOGUE

The Hughes family has set up a scholarship fund at De La Salle High School in John's name. Every year they hold a golf outing to help fund it. They remember their lost son and brother with love. The memory of him can bring instant tears. After more than four decades, the loss is in many ways still fresh.

They have a website for the fund that carries these words:

John's legacy as a leader began during his grade school years at St. Gabriel in Canaryville, most notably when he first donned a helmet to play for the Shamrocks—a squad coached by his Uncle, Stephen Patrick Hughes. Dubbed "Big Red" by his teammates, after John honed his skills at St. Gabriel he went on to play football in high school, excelling at the game for the De La Salle Meteors. He was an outstanding defensive back who helped lead the freshman squad to an undefeated season, and continued to be a hard-hitting competitive force throughout his sophomore and junior years.

John was a leader off the gridiron as well. He made the honor roll quarter after quarter and was involved in several extracurricular activities, including student government. During his junior year, before his young life ended tragically, he served as De La Salle's student body vice president, and John's friends, family and teammates believe, beyond a shadow of a doubt, that John would have been the student body president as a senior.

The De La Salle family will miss him most dearly because of who he was as a person. Even more than his academic and athletic exploits, John will be remembered for his charisma, sense of humor, fortitude and compassion.

Nick Costello declined to comment for this project through his law-yer, who noted Costello has repeatedly denied any involvement. The attorney said Costello on one occasion gave his version of events to a grand jury, an appearance Sherlock found no record of.

LaMantia's attorney at the time of the Hughes and Martha DiCaro killings, Anthony J. Onesto, said he could not speak to the Hughes slaying or any alleged LaMantia role in it, and that he did not specifically recall the incident. He called Martha DiCaro's death a "tragic, tragic case," and said it was likely some kind of acci-dent. As for information that Shorty LaMantia could have paid off the judge at the time, Onesto was dismissive of the idea. "It's easy to throw rocks at a guy like Shorty, because he's not going to respond," Onesto told the author. "Whatever he was, he was."

A close relative of LaMantia's, when reached by the author, declined to address the news that an investigator with the FBI was looking into LaMantia's suspected involvement in the Hughes case.

EPILOGUE

Reached by the author, Paul Ferraro also declined to comment on the case, saying he knew nothing about it.

Bridgeport is changing. Its proximity to downtown Chicago has made it attractive to young professionals who initially were drawn to its cheaper housing stock. They gather for parties at some of the old standbys but have put their own stamp on places like Maria's Packaged Goods and Community Bar. White Sox Park is now named for some kind of mortgage company, and the team markets itself to young families. The neighborhood's location near Chicago's traditional Chinese neighborhood on the near South Side has also meant a larger influence of that community in Bridgeport, as Chinatown has essentially overflowed and Chinese businesses have gone looking for new areas to set up shop. All of the new growth and a younger demographic has meant some of the neighborhood's traditional walls have come down. It is in some ways less insular. And there are fusion restaurants now, and ones offering herbal Rishi tea and avocado fries.

As for Canaryville, it has not experienced the same upscale turn. But whatever the Chicago of the future might be, the neighborhood may still take a place in it as more than just a museum piece of the city's past. It is still proud of its blue-collar roots, but it too has seen movement away from its history as a closed-off slice of the city with an often-deserved reputation for racism and tribal thinking. The neighborhood, and areas around it, have lately grown more integrated.

Jim Sherlock did join the Cook County state's attorney's office in 2020. His work included assisting with cold cases.

In fact, in the fall of 2020, Sherlock drove back to Sandwich to tell Costello that he was not fully retired, and that the case would stay on his mind and on his new desk. If Costello would speak to him, there was still a path to doing the right thing. There had been some thought about whistling Costello to the FBI building in Chicago for potential questioning, as some agents thought there was enough probable cause to at least bring him in. Ultimately that plan was abandoned, as Sherlock and those he worked with believed it would only cause Costello to bring in his lawyer and perhaps seal off that route for good.

Instead, Sherlock decided again on a soft sell. He didn't announce he was coming, and arrived to find that Costello wasn't at home. He spoke to the man's wife, delivering his message and leaving hopeful that maybe the woman could convince her husband to share the truth about what happened and move on with his life. But it was not to be. A few days later, Sherlock was faxed a letter from Costello's lawyer again declining to make him available and requesting that any future requests go through the lawyer's office.

As Sherlock dug into his new job, he had a conversation with a CPD detective who worked cold cases, and brought him up to speed on the Hughes investigation. The two discussed locking in the accounts of Larry Raddatz and Mary Mestrovic Murrihy before a Cook County grand jury, and perhaps eventually granting Costello full immunity, compelling his testimony and overriding any Fifth Amendment claim. But obstacles remained, including grand jury activity being slowed by the coronavirus pandemic and the need for Sherlock to get the full commitment of the state's attorney's office.

Sherlock's old team, CE-6 at the FBI, made headlines in late 2018 with a sweeping racketeering case against the Goonie Boss street gang, a faction of Chicago's powerful Gangster Disciples. The gang had run roughshod through Englewood, racking up some eleven murders.

The investigation was such a success, it led local FBI leaders to think the unit needed its own space, somewhere away from the main FBI Chicago headquarters on Roosevelt Road near Western Avenue. One of the considerations was having closer access to the South Side areas like the ones they had worked in the Goonie Boss investigation. Something really local.

Among the spaces they looked at using was the old Ninth District police station at Thirty-Fifth and Lowe, the building so heavily linked to the Hughes case, where police leaders took over interviews and took Mary Mestrovic's statement out of the hands of detectives in 1976. The FBI looked at the space, shuffling through dust and peeling paint. Paperwork was left on tables and desks, remaining in the places it sat when the last Chicago cops walked out and the building was abandoned.

It had taken a star turn once before.

The old police district was featured in a brief scene in the 1948 classic black-and-white movie *Call Northside 777*, a film noir that starred Jimmy Stewart as a snappy Chicago newspaper reporter chasing the truth about a 1932 murder of a cop in a speakeasy in the waning months of Prohibition. The film mirrored an actual case of a wrongful conviction based on a bad identification by a witness.

Just before Stewart's character P. J. McNeal heads to the Ninth District building, which is playing the part of the New City police district in the movie, he calls into the station, acting as if he's a ranking officer at CPD headquarters.

He asks the cop who answers the phone whether an arrest report is there on the man who was charged and convicted, a poor sap named Frank Wiecek.

The fake-out works. Yes, the cop answers, the report is there. And Stewart is just in time. An unnamed someone had already directed officers in the station to do something with it.

That direction, the cop says to McNeal, was to remove the paperwork from their files.

ACKNOWLEDGMENTS

This project simply does not happen without Jim Sherlock, whose work on the Hughes case is the central thread of this story. Thank you, Jim, for trusting me to tell the tale of your effort, and thank you for the help you provided in so many ways. I will always remember getting to know you as part of this project. I owe you more than one trip to Cafe Bionda.

Thank you very much to the Hughes family, in particular Ellen Hughes Morrissey, for welcoming me into your home. A special thanks as well to Mary Mestrovic Murrihy, for taking the step of talking to yet another unknown person about your experiences.

Thank you as well to Terry Strong, John Raddatz, and Brian O'Malley for taking the time to relate your memories.

Special thanks to Nuccio DiNuzzo, a former *Chicago Tribune* photographer who did work on this project and took the author photo.

I'd also of course like to thank my family and friends for their support of this project. In particular I would like to thank my wife Tracy. Work like this usually places stress on other parts of an author's life, both at home and at work, and this was no different. That situation was not helped by the fact that as the writing was coming together, Tracy was preparing to give birth to our daughter, Sloane. Thank you, Trace, for tolerating me and the nights and weekends in front of a laptop and for everything else. And thanks, Sloanie Macaroni, for the hard work of occasionally taking a nap.

Thanks also to my mother-in-law Lisa, for all of the support and help with our new family and for being there for us always. Also thank you to Meredith and Liam for your love always and to my parents, Doug and Kathy Coen. Thanks to Chris and Mike, Jeremy and Denise, and Vince Cook for their support as well.

Thank you to my colleagues at the *Chicago Tribune*, where I have now spent more than twenty years of my professional life. Thanks especially to Peter Kendall, a former editor, and other management there for the allowance to produce this book. Thanks to my often partner Stacy St. Clair for your friendship. Thank you to my friends on "the String."

Thank you also to those who assisted me in getting certain public documents needed for the project, in particular Joseph Fitzpatrick of the US attorney's office in Chicago, for help with federal court records.

And thanks, finally, to my friends at Chicago Review Press. Cynthia Sherry, the publisher there, can now be counted as a longtime supporter. Thanks for taking my calls on this and for having faith in it. And thank you to my editor, Kara Rota. Your thoughts and guidance were essential to making this work.

ADDITIONAL REFERENCES

Most references, including books, newspaper stories, official reports, and other materials, are cited by name at the appropriate point in the text, but not all. Here is a list of other helpful books, articles, and publications that influenced and informed this work. The author is thankful for the efforts of so many great writers and reporters who have informed Chicagoans about their city for so long.

Belluck, Pam. "Top Chicago Police Official Will Retire over Disclosure." *New York Times*, November 15, 1997.

Cole, Patrick. "Key Cop with Longtime Clout to Retire from Chicago Force." *Chicago Tribune*, February 1, 2000.

Dyja, Thomas. *The Third Coast: When Chicago Built the American Dream*. New York: Penguin Books, 2013.

Farr, Finis. *Chicago: A Personal History of America's Most American City*. New Rochelle, NY: Arlington House Publishers, 1973.

Garmes, Kyle. "Haberkorn, 94, Tough, Loyal Cop, Loving Family Man." *Beverly Review*, May 22, 2018.

Gorman, John. "Court Told of Mob-Negotiated Gambling 'Tax.'" *Chicago Tribune*, April 12, 1991.

Gorner, Jeremy, and Annie Sweeney. "William Hanhardt: 1928–2016; Ex-Cop Convicted of Running Jewel Theft Operation." *Chicago Tribune*, December 31, 2016.

ADDITIONAL REFERENCES

Hinkel, Dan. "CPD Misses Deadlines on Reforms." *Chicago Tribune*, November 16, 2019.

Lombardo, Robert. *Organized Crime in Chicago: Beyond the Mafia.* Urbana, IL: University of Illinois Press, 2013.

Pacyga, Dominic. *Chicago: A Biography.* Chicago: University of Chicago Press, 2009.

Pascente, Fred, and Sam Reaves. *Mob Cop: My Life of Crime in the Chicago Police Department.* Chicago: Chicago Review Press, 2015.

Police Accountability Task Force. "Recommendations for Reform: Restoring Trust Between the Chicago Police and the Communities They Serve." April 2016.

Sobol, Rosemary, Jeremy Gorner, and David Heinzmann. "Jon Burge: 1947–2018; Disgraced Officer Long Tied to Torture." *Chicago Tribune*, September 20, 2018.

Stein, Sharman. "Canaryville Beatings Prompt 2 Cop Firings." *Chicago Tribune*, March 21, 1992.

United States Department of Justice Civil Rights Division and United States Attorney's Office Northern District of Illinois. "Investigation of the Chicago Police Department." January 13, 2017.